LINGUISTICS

F O R B E G I N N E R S ®

LINGUISTICS

FOR BEGINNERS

BY **W. TERRENCE GORDON**
ILLUSTRATIONS BY **SUSAN WILLMARTH**

FOR BEGINNERS®

For Beginners LLC
155 Main Street, Suite 211
Danbury, CT 06810 USA
www.forbeginnersbooks.com

Text: © 2008 W. Terrence Gordon
Illustrations: © 2008 Susan Willmarth
Cover Art: © 2008 Susan Willmarth

A For Beginners® Documentary Comic Book
Copyright © 2008

Cataloging-in-Publication information is available from
the Library of Congress.

ISBN-10 # 1-934389-28-5 Trade
ISBN-13 # 978-1-934389-28-7 Trade

Manufactured in the United States of America

For Beginners® and Beginners Documentary Comic Books®
are published by For Beginners LLC.

Reprint Edition

If you have already heard about linguistics or read something about the subject, and you share the feeling that Ogden Nash describes above, you've come to the right book. If you know nothing at all about the topic but have picked up this book out of sheer curiosity, so much the better. Read on, and take your first steps toward learning what linguists do for a living.

HOW LANGUAGES WORK

Lessons One and Two

Let's start with these basics:

**language is a tool;
linguistics is the analysis of language**

Why say that language is a tool? Because like any of the things that we recognize as tools, from hammers to computers, it lets us do things that would otherwise be impossible or a lot harder to do (try to imagine driving nails without a hammer or compiling a city phone directory without the help of a computer).

Language is a tool for getting thoughts out of our brains and into our mouths and into other brains.

How else would we communicate? Sure, you can just let out a yell to warn of danger, or a groan to express pain, strain, or boredom, and a map or a sketch can give a lot of information. But try sketching this:

I'll never forget her laugh.

Apart from "laugh," the elements of this sentence are too abstract for a picture. They are ideas and concepts, expressible only when organized *by* and *into* a complex system: language.

AH-HO-HA-HA-HE-HE-HE

Unlike most other tools, language can be used on itself, and that is exactly what happens in the study called *linguistics.* It is analysis of language, it is language about language.

Here's another way to think about it: linguistics is to language what a mechanic's manual is to a car. A linguist working on a language with analytical tools is not much different from a mechanic working on an engine with his socket wrenches. The shop manual is not a driver education handbook, and a book on linguistics does not teach you how to speak. It's possible to be a competent mechanic without knowing how to drive a car and just as possible to be a linguist without being fluent in the language you are analyzing. (More about this below, where we meet three guys names Chomsky, Mithridates, and Fazah.)

What? No Words?

So far, we haven't said a word about words, and we're not defining linguistics as words about words. Why? Because **linguistic analysis is not limited to words.**

Linguistics goes below and above the word. It takes words apart (*hopelessly=hope+less+ly*) and examines how the parts go together (*hope+less+ly* but not *less+hope+ly*). It also looks at how words form groups (*He is hopelessly lost* but not *Lost is hopelessly he*).

When a sentence makes sense, its words are linked like pearls on a string. What keeps the words together is a pattern. Many different sets of pearls could be put together on the same piece of string, and many different sets of words can hang together on the same pattern. The study of patterns for sentences is called *syntax* by linguists and *grammar* by the rest of the world. Let's go back to our example: He is hopelessly lost.

This sentence has the same pattern (we could also say *the same model* or *the same structure*, and we will see later that *structure* especially is a favorite word among linguists) as the following:

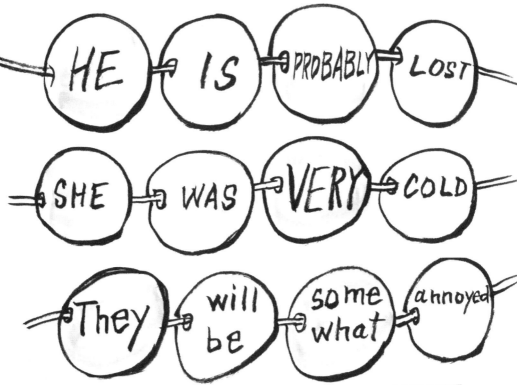

He is probably lost.
She was very cold.
They will be somewhat annoyed.

Linguists are a lot less interested in words than they are in how words combine with each other and in how bits and pieces combine to make up a word. The bits and pieces of spoken language turn out to be more interesting

SHE WAS VERY COLD

SHE WAS VERY COLD

than those of written language, because there is more regularity, more system, more pattern, more structure (there's that linguist's word or choice again) in speech than in writing. Think of it this way: you can line up ten people who all look very different from each other, but if you line up their x-rays, their skeletons will look very similar. Linguists pay more attention to skeletons than to skin; they spend more time studying the sounds of speech and sound systems than words on the page.

Put it in Writing

But let's not imagine that learning about writing is completely outside the important fundamentals of linguistics. We write English in what is called a *phonetic alphabet*. This means that the letters of the alphabet stand for sounds, the most basic elements of language that linguists study.

A phonetic alphabet is a medium, in the sense of an extension of our bodies. It turns the sounds of language that we produce with our lungs and tongues and teeth and lips into visual marks, whereas the sounds of language are an extension of the thoughts in our minds. Here we are back at the basic idea we started with: language as a tool.

A phonetic alphabet is a tool or medium not only because it extends our bodies but in the even more basic sense of something that goes between and brings together. What does a phonetic alphabet go between and bring together? Meaning and sound.

If we compare, say, Chinese characters, with a phonetic alphabet, we find no "go-between" in Chinese. The writing gives meanings, but it doesn't show how to pronounce what is written.

If you are having trouble understanding this, think about symbols like + or $ or %. There is nothing in the shapes of these symbols to show how they are pronounced, but there is in the letters of *plus, dollar,* and *percent.* Imagine if every word in English was a symbol like + instead of *plus,* $ instead of *dollar,* or % instead of *percent,* and then you've got an idea of how Chinese works and how it is different from a phonetic alphabet.

What Does a Linguist Do from Nine to Five?

Some linguists study one language and how its sounds vary in different places in a sound-group (*p*, for example, is not pronounced in exactly the same way at the beginning of a word in English—*pot*, and at the end—*top*). Some may examine the street slang of their own neighborhoods, but others may race to a far corner of the world to record conversations among the last few speakers of a dying language.

This is all modern linguistics, twentieth century linguistics, as it has been practiced since the time of Swiss scholar Ferdinand de Saussure (1857-1913) and because of his influence. So far-reaching has this influence been that Saussure is often called the father of modern linguistics. But what about earlier?

Is it not possible that people have been thinking about language for almost as long as they have been using it? In fact, we find the first flowering of linguistic thought twenty-two centuries before Saussure.

Ferdinand de Saussure

The French word *linguistique* had already been in use for at least 24 years when Saussure was born; its English cousin *linguistic* appeared first in 1837 in the writings of the British scholar William Whewell, who defined it as the science of language. Under the influence of American scholars such as

Dwight Whitney

Noah Webster and Dwight Whitney, *linguistic* was transformed into *linguistics*.

By comparison with *linguistic(s)*, *linguist* has a much longer history, having been used first by Shakespeare in 1591 in *Two Gentlemen of Verona* to mean "one who is skilled in the use of language." Language scholars were known as *philologists* before *linguist* came along, and the two terms continued in use alongside each other through the years of Saussure's lifetime.

What does a linguist not do at any time of day? The job of the linguist is to describe language, to record it, analyze it, explain how it works, theorize about how we learn it, and much more. But not to dictate how you should use your language. That would be just as inappropriate as a geneticist giving you suggestions about who you should mate with. But of course there are cases where there has been meddling and mending...

POLICIES AND POLICE, PROTOCOL AND POLITICS:
The Linguistic Mix

1) Saussure taught that language change comes about spontaneous-ly and cannot be imposed, but this has not kept any number of people from trying, and their efforts are sometimes called *linguistic engineering*. At its worst, the phenomenon can induce collective brainwashing (*Newspeak* in George Orwell's *1984*); at its best it eliminates prejudice and bias, as in the introduction of *Down's syndrome* to replace *mongolism*, *engender* to replace *father* (pseudogeneric verb), or *founder* to replace *father* (pseudogeneric noun).

2) In Canada, Quebec's Commission de la protection de la langue française (Commission for Protection of the French Language) is commonly known in English as the *language police*. It is the business of this body to enforce Quebec's parochial and misguided legislation for ensuring the survival of the French language in the predominant-ly French-speaking province (words on public signs in languages other than French must be half the size of French words). The language police have been vigilant enough to spot unilingual English matzo meal packaging. And, a Montreal gravestone maker has been required to downsize the Hebrew lettering on a fifty year old sign over his business premises.

3) Modern society is making progress toward eliminating language that is prejudicial against persons because of their race, sex, age, sexual orientation, disability, ethnic origin, or belief system. But linguists and non-linguists alike disagree on exactly where to draw the line on what is deemed to be biased language. Is *fellowship* objectionable? Should a new term be invented for a female holder of a fellowship? It is true that the primary meaning of the root word *fellow* given in most dictionaries is that of *man or boy*, but historically there are several other meanings such as *associate, companion, trustee, etc.,* and the Old English origin of the term is a gender free word for *business partner*. Of course, it is possible to argue that in contexts where the meanings of *associate, companion, etc.,* are to be expressed, one should opt for one of these terms. And it is probably true that even if Old English *feolaga* (*business partner*) was technically gender-free, there were probably few if any female business partners to be found a thousand years ago!

CHOMKSY, FAZAH, AND MITHRIDATES (NOT A LAW FIRM)

If you have read anything about linguistics, you may have already discovered that the name of *Noam Chomsky* has dominated the field, particularly in the United States, for fifty years. Chomsky is credited with recharting the course of linguistics when, with the ink still fresh on his Ph.D. from the University of Pennsylvania, he published *Syntactic Structures* in 1957. It was a very slim book but enough of a fire-cracker to start linguists arguing about **how** they should approach the analysis of language. They are still at it. Linguistics has gone through many phases of development as a direct result of Chomsky's work (as have his own basic ideas on the subject).

SAUSSURE

Is Chomsky the greatest linguist on the planet?

Not so, says the *Guinness Book of World Records*, where the top contender for the title is one Ziad Fazah of Brazil, who speaks and writes 58 languages.

CHOMSKY

History records that one of the first persons known for his multilingual skills was King Mithridates of Pontus (132-63 B.C.E.), who was fluent in 22 languages.

The *Guinness Book* uses *linguist* in the sense we saw earlier, as per Shakespeare: one who knows many languages. Apparently, in that respect, Dr. Chomsky can't hold a candle to King Mithridates, much less to Mr. Fazah.

Linguistics Then and Now

It didn't take the invention of the terms *linguist* and *linguistics* for the analytic study of language to begin. The link between logic and language goes back to ancient times in Aristotle's work and the categories he set up mark the beginnings of what would eventually be called *linguistics*.

The logic/language connection is still important to linguists today. When computers came on the scene, after the Second World War, somebody soon got the idea to try using them for translating. To do this, it was necessary to give the computer information about the languages it would translate in terms of very basic logic. So, logical and mathematical models of language began to appear, and they have dominated linguistics ever since.

Input ≠ Output

The story goes that the first experiment in translation by computer (usually called machine translation, even though the computer is not a machine in the usual sense of having mechanical parts) was not a success. Supposedly an international team of linguists and translators had worked long and hard and thought that they had everything ready to get their computer to translate from English to Japanese. They gave it the sentence "The spirit is willing, but the flesh is weak." The translation did not take long, but unfortunately it came out meaning "The drink is all right, but the meat is lousy." So it was back to the drawing board.

*****

It's easy enough to get a computer to recognize a sentence pattern but very difficult to give it all the details about the limits of the pattern. All human languages have patterns, because humans have pattern-making minds, but language patterns are incomplete, imperfect, irregular in all kinds of ways:

sing-sang-sung and *ring-rang-rung*

sink-sank-sunk but not *think-thank-thunk*

and definitely not *pink-pank-punk*

horror-horrid-horrify is a complete pattern

terror-terrify, candor-candid are incomplete patterns

These incomplete patterns are no problem for us; we learn what and where the quirks are. It's a big problem for a computer to "understand" that you can *have a smoke* or *have a drink* but you can't *have an eat. (In linguistics, an asterisk precedes a word or phrase that is not found in standard use. This once prompted a linguist to come up with the rallying cry: *Linguists of the world unite; you have nothing but your asterisk.*) So *terrid, *candify.

HAVE A DRINK

HAVE A SMOKE

can't HAVE AN EAT

More About Writing it Down

Let's come back to three points we've already touched on and tie them together: 1) Linguists are especially interested in the bits and pieces of language; 2) the average linguist is more likely to pay attention to the stream of speech coming out of somebody's mouth than to chunks of language flash-frozen in written words; 3) We write English in an alphabet that shows us how to pronounce our words.

PHONETIC STRUCTURE

night [nait]

WORD STRUCTURE   HOPE   LESS   LY

SENTENCE STRUCTURE   HE   IS   HOPELESSLY   LOST

Think about this last statement. It is only partly true. The first letter in *knight, gnome,* and *psyche,* for example, *does not* tell us what the first sound in the word is. In the long history of English, the written language has not kept up with the changes that have taken place in speech. So, we have words where different letters stand for the same sound (*way, weigh, whey*) and words where the same letter stands for different sounds (the *o* in *on, once, onion, only*). And then there are combinations of letters that represent only one sound (*th, sh,* for example) and those silent letters in *knight, gnome, psychic,* etc.

talking proper   talking posh

Received Pronunciation

This phrase refers to the pronunciation of Received Standard English, the most prestigious dialect of British English—a class dialect rather than a local dialect, though it is associated primarily with the southern counties. "RP," as it is commonly known, is used by highly educated Britons and members of the Establishment. It is also known as *the BBC accent, the public school accent, talking proper,* and *talking posh.*

Talking Posh

An English professor complained to the owner of the pet shop where he had recently bought a parrot: "He uses improper language."

"Well, I am surprised," replied the shopkeeper, "I never taught him to swear."

"Oh, it's not that," explained the professor, "but he keeps splitting his infinitives."

And Still More About Writing it Down

English is not the only language with inconsistent spelling or silent letters. In French, to take just one example, the verb *avoir*, meaning *to have*, has many forms, including *aies*. Here the four letters stand for just one sound. The word is pronounced like the vowel *e* in English *pet*.

The muddled up spellings of languages like English or French forced linguists to invent a new way of writing down speech to show it accurately and consistently. It is called the *International Phonetic Alphabet (IPA)*. Here are some of the words we have already used as examples transposed into the IPA:

night      [nait]

The column on the right shows the way that Henry Higgins recorded Eliza Doolittle's way of speaking English in his notebook in the opening scene of *My Fair Lady*.

Knight      [nait]

Those square brackets indicate a **phonetic** transcription — a written record of somebody talking. If I'm speaking very quickly and use the word "only," I may pronounce it [oni], and if a linguist is taking down my words, she will transcribe [oni] not [onli] to show exactly what I said.

gnome      [noum]

NOAM

psychic   [saikik]

way	[wei]
on	[ɔn]
once	[wʌns]
onion	[ʌnjʌn]
only	[ounli]
(French) aies	[ɛ]

[19

Of course, in spite of my little slip, I know the usual pronunciation of the word, and if this is what the linguist wants to show, forward slashes are used around the transcription instead of square brackets: /onli/. Now we have an example of what is called **phonemic** or **phonological** transcription—not one person's words but what people usually say. Here we are moving up from the particulars of speech (**phonetics**) to the patterns and system of sounds of language (**phonology**).

If all this talk about **phonetics** and **phonology** has inspired you already to become a modern-day Henry (or Henrietta) Higgins, you can start by going to the section further on here titled "More About Phonetics."

Introducing Sammy Mansfield

Most textbooks of linguistics present a chapter on **phonetics** and **phonology** with a diagram of a cut-away head to show the organs of speech and the place of articulation of speech sounds. The diagram is a (presumably) male head and always shown from the left side. This fellow is called Sammy Mansfield, and his name is a link, via the initials, to what the diagram represents: Speech Mechanism. (The corresponding phrase in French is *appareil de production sonore* or *organes articulatoires*, but efforts to standardize the name of Sammy's French counterpart as either *Albert Philippe Simard* or *Odette Arsenault*—the latter a particular admirable effort to counter the male bias too often encountered in the old bastions of Gallic culture—have met with only limited success.) Here is Sammy...or Alphonse...or Odette.

Incidentally, most versions of this diagram show the talking head (you've never seen one like this on TV) with nostrils blocked, which would make it tough (to say the least) to produce nasal sounds. In the interest of accuracy, and to make life easier for Sammy, we show him unblocked.

Quantum Leap #1 –
Breaking the Sound Barrier

Every language is a self-contained system. (By *system* we mean a set of elements and rules for their use.) Sounds that make a difference in meaning in one language may not work the same way in another. We can start with English *veal* and *wheel* to illustrate this point. Words like these are called *minimal pairs*. They are the conjoined twins of language. Just one sound in each is different from one sound in the other. If we compare Ukrainian (a Slavic language), we do not find any minimal pairs similar to *veal/wheel*.

Minimal pairs provide linguists with the evidence of the units they call **phonemes** - the sounds of language whose job it is to allow different meanings. The **phonemes** that make up the English sound system (English **phonology**) include /v/ and /w/; in Ukrainian there are many words that begin with /v/ but none that begin with /w/. There are also Ukrainian words that end in /w/ but none that end in /v/. So two sounds that are separate **phonemes** in English belong to the same **phoneme** in Ukrainian, where there are no pairs of words contrasting in meaning comparable to English *veal/ wheel*.

PHONEMES

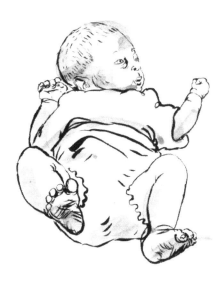

We learn the **phonemes** of our first language without knowing what a **phoneme** is or how it works. (You can learn to drive a car without being a mechanic or even knowing the principle of the combustion engine.) We carry over the habits we acquired in mastering our first language when we approach a new one and can soon bump up against a few problems with **phonemes** that refuse to behave like the ones we are familiar with. This is why a Ukrainian speaker learning English will say [vel] for *well*, [vik] for *week*, etc.

Quantum Leap #2 – Passing the Cranberry Test

At this point, most books on linguistics march you straight from **phonology** to long lessons on *morphology*, from a language's system of sounds (which mean nothing in themselves) to the way they work to communicate meaning. Here we'll limit ourselves to introducing *morphology* by way of some facts about the phrase *cranberry linguist*. But first a word about our new word *morphology*.

Morphology comes from the Greek noun meaning *form*, the same root word that we find in *metamorphosis* (change of form), *morphogenesis* (structural changes in the evolution and development of an organism), and even *Morpheus* (in Greek mythology, the god of sleep, so called because of the *forms* or *shapes* that he calls up in dreams).

Linguists are not the only group of specialists to use the term *morphology*. For scholars in other disciplines, it refers to the study of form and structure of plants, animals, human bones, continents, etc. In linguistics, it means *the study of the smallest forms that carry meaning*. These forms are called *morphemes*.

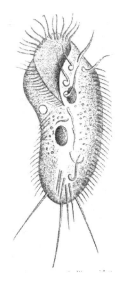

They do not have to be words; they can be part of a word, as long as that part gives some meaning. *In* is a *morpheme* and a word, *direct* is a *morpheme* and a word, *indirect* is two *morphemes* but only one word. The *in-* at the beginning of *indirect*, carrying the meaning of *not*, is not the *morpheme*/word *in* (opposite of *out*). Think about the difference between *in direct communication* and *indirect communication*.

We can think of *morphology* as the part of linguistics that links **phonology** (the study of the functional sounds of language) and **syntax** (the study of arrangements of meaningful forms) by identifying those meaningful forms.

Now for that *cranberry linguist*. This is actually a term of contempt among linguists for one of their number who studies nothing more important than the *morphology* of *cranberry* and the question of where the *cran-* in *cranberry* comes from. (It is a variation on *crane*, one explanation being that cranberries typically grow in marshy land of the kind cranes favor for nesting. Not all linguists—cranberry and non-cranberry alike—favor this hypothesis: it has also been suggested that the Pilgrims called the fruit *craneberry* because its arching blossoms suggested the shape of the bird. So disagreement is over the motivation for *crane*, rather than the *crane/cran-* alternation, which is typical of a substantial number of pairs of related words: *sane/sanity, urbane/urbanity, profane/profanity,* etc. Before *cranberry* was imported into British English from America, both plant and fruit were known in England as *marsh-whort, fen-whort, fen-berry, marshberry,* and *mossberry.* In German, Swedish, Danish, and other continental languages, the term for *cranberry* is a compound word and a direct translation of *craneberry.*)

Quantum Leap #3 - Clusterings beyond the Cranberries

We move on now from *morphology* to **syntax**. This term comes from Greek syn (together) + tassein (to arrange).

In **phonology**, **phonemes** are arranged together,

and the arrangements create the simple units of meaning called *morphemes*;

CAT

in **syntax**, *morphemes* are arranged together,

and the arrangements create the complex units of meaning called *phrases* and *sentences*.

TABBY CAT

Phonology, *morphology*, and **syntax** are different levels of analysis. Linguists separate elements of language at these levels for purposes of analysis, but in practice no such separation occurs.

(You can't drive your car if the carburetor is sitting on the workbench in your garage.)

Linguistics manuals often give a diagram for an overview of the subject with *morphology* stacked on top of ***phonology***, **syntax** stacked on top of *morphology*, and **semantics** (meaning) at the very top of the pile, as if you don't get to meaning till you have worked your way "up" through the other levels.

Not so! Sure, we can just make a list of the ***phonemes*** of a language, but even in doing that we are indicating the sounds that work together to create meaning. When language functions, ***phonology*** is inseparable from **semantics**, *morphology* is inseparable from ***phonology***, **syntax** is inseparable from *morphology*, etc.

SYNTAX

morphology

PHONOLOGY

Semantics is the messiest level of linguistics, because the human mind is good at making and multiplying meanings and because the resources of language for doing this are very complex. So before we tackle **semantics**, let's get **syntax** (where things are a little tidier— at least at the entry level) out of the way.

When computers came into general use after World War II, their potential for endless applications soon became apparent, and these included translation. This requires supplying the computer with enough information to be able to recognize how sentences can change form without changing meaning (Example: *The fireman rescued the cat; The cat was rescued by the fireman*).

Describing the relation of different forms of a sentence to each other is known as transformational **syntax** (or *transformational grammar,* and here we have to remember that *grammar* means not just rules for sentence construction, and especially not rules for constructing "good" sentences, since linguists abstain from such value judgments, but simply a description of how language works. Though transformational **syntax** was first developed for use in machine translation, it soon took on a life of its own and changed the face of modern linguistic theory.

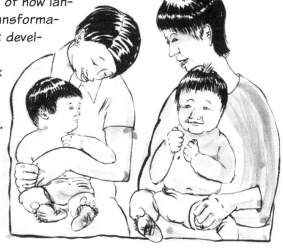

Transformational **syntax** is also known as *generative* **syntax** (or *generative grammar*). It is a theoretical framework for viewing language as an infinite set of potential sentences which may be *generated* from a finite set of abstract rules and principles. In other words, when we know a language, we know how to put together an unlimited number of new sentences from a limited set of rules. We acquire this amazing skill as children by listening to adults talking at us and figuring out what the rules are that will let us talk back to them in such a way as to make ourselves understood.

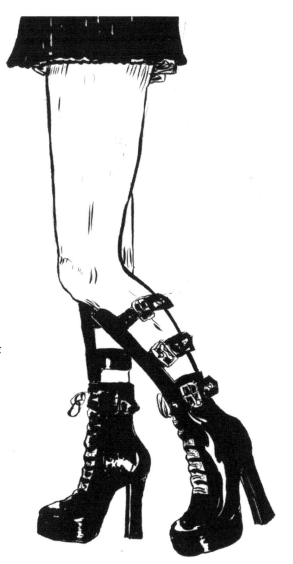

Linguistic Fun: Rhyming Slang

Cockney in origin, this form of slang replaces a word by a phrase that rhymes with it but suppresses the rhyming part. Thus, "kid," rhyming with "God forbid," turns "How are the kids?" into "How are the godfors?" "Legs" rhymes with "bacon and eggs," and so "She's go smashing legs" becomes "She's got smashing bacons." It takes a while to get the crash-boom of it.

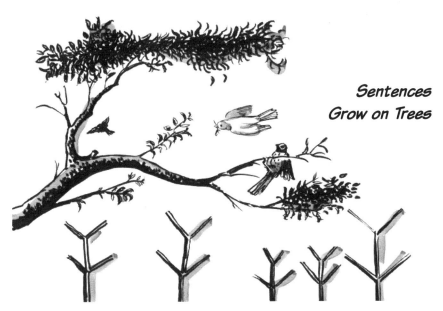

Sentences Grow on Trees

At least in linguistics they do. What's more, the trees grow upside down. *Tree*, in this case, is the name given to a diagram for the steps and stages in the production of a sentence. In keeping with the image of a tree, we could also call these steps and stages the *growth* or the *development* of a sentence. The term *derivation*, in this sense, is particularly favored by linguists. So the linguist's tree is a visual help for showing the particulars of a sentence. Branch by branch.

Naturally we are going to give only simple examples here, so don't expect the tree diagrams to look very much like an inverted version of that magnificent oak outside your window. For one thing, it doesn't have any leaves. Our tree here grows into a fully-formed structure, branching from a seed that already contains the whole sentence, but the growth is limited to the branching itself.

The only "blossoms" you will find on these tree diagrams are words that can take their place at the final stage of its growth. Before we get to that stage, we find branching points labeled with initials that stand for the type of phrase that occurs there: *NP* (noun phrase), *VP* (verb phrase), *PP* (prepositional phrase), etc., all stemming from *S* (sentence).

Here is a derivational tree for the sentence *Thomas ate the fruit in the kitchen.*

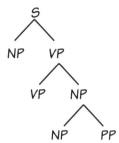

You may wonder why the diagram always shows phrases, implying groups of words, when some of the elements of our sample sentence are single words: the *NP* subject of the sentence is just *Thomas* and the *VP* is the simple verb form *ate*. Well, it's because our tree needs to be general enough to accommodate sentences that follow the same pattern as *Thomas ate the fruit in the kitchen*, and many of these will turn out to have complex elements. (These would be shown in more detail in an expanded diagram.)

The same tree lets us diagram the sentence *Charles's favorite uncle eventually gobbled up all the apples, oranges, and bananas in the room adjacent to the dining room.* Our page isn't big enough to show the full tree for this sentence, but the basic tree for it is the same as the one we have already.

We can see that two or more sentences (in fact an unlimited number of sentences) will have the same tree structure. But one sentence can also have two or more tree diagrams associated with it. In fact, that is the case for *Thomas ate the fruit in the kitchen.* In setting out the diagram for this sentence, we assumed something about its meaning, namely that the fruit was in the kitchen before Thomas ate it.

We don't really know from the sentence itself if he was in the kitchen when he ate it, but this is one possibility; there is a strong suggestion for the same interpretation of the sentence that there was fruit in another room that Thomas could have eaten instead. But if we know for sure that Thomas did the eating in the kitchen, we need a different tree diagram to show this:

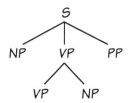

The basic difference between our two trees is that the *PP* (Prepositional phrase) in the second is independent of the *second NP* (*the fruit*), whereas it was directly linked to it in the first case. Now it occurs in the first branching of the tree, and this puts it in direct relation to the *first NP*, indicating in this way that Thomas was in the kitchen when he ate the fruit. (This time we don't know for sure if he found the fruit there or got it somewhere else and was just eating it in the kitchen so that the people in the other room wouldn't see what a pig he was making of himself.)

In a more detailed analysis important differences emerge from such features and contrasts as **right-branching sentences**:

> This is the cat that caught the rat that ate the cheese that lay in the trap...

and **left-branching sentences**:

> The racing car's driver's side door's number decal's paint job's color's...

Even though we are just at a very elementary stage of learning about generative **syntax**, we can see already that sentence structure and meaning interact. This becomes even clearer when we move on from the derivation of a sentence to its transformation. For our sample, the two meanings have to be distinguished when the sentence is turned into a passive construction:

The fruit in the kitchen was eaten by Charles (tree #1)

vs.

The fruit was eaten in the kitchen by Charles (tree #2)

or

The fruit was eaten by Charles in the kitchen (tree #2)

If you understood all this with no problem, it's because you are coming to it from inside the world's most efficient and complex communication system, even though it is made up mostly of salty water—the human body with its built-in mind. Computers can't understand anything unless it is laid out for them step by step and they can't make the choices we make in understanding and using language without instructions to make them one at a time.

WORLD'S MOST TRIVIAL PIECE OF LINGUIST-RELATED INFORMATION:

The father of American linguist Benjamin Lee Whorf (1897-1941), a commercial artist, designed a figure that has been in use continuously for nearly a century – the cap-and-clog-clad lass on the label of Old Dutch cleanser.

Tree diagrams and everything else that belongs to the apparatus of generative **syntax** is the legacy of the original scheme to use computers to translate human languages. We can see at a glance the difference between the tree diagrams for the two interpretations of *Thomas ate the fruit in the kitchen*; a computer can't see anything and can only get the difference by beavering away at a series of two-way choices—the branching points of our tree diagrams.

Before we let Thomas alone to digest his fruit, let's notice another point in this example that is of interest to linguists. We have pretty well nailed down the *ambiguity* (more than one possible meaning) of the sentence, the different sentence structures associated with those possibilities, and the contrasts that show up when the different interpretations are paraphrased as passives. But there is still a lot we do not know and cannot know from the sentence, from its structure, or from its words.

If we compare the sentence about Thomas with the one about Charles's favorite uncle, there seem to be similarities beyond the basic one that lets us diagram both with the same tree. *Ate* is a less colorful and less specific version of *eventually gobbled up all, the fruit* corresponds to *apples, oranges, and bananas* as category to members, but after that things get a little fuzzier. Can we be sure that *the kitchen* refers to the room adjacent to the dining room? It doesn't have to. Is Thomas Charles's favorite uncle? There is certainly no reason to assume so (though I will tell you confidentially that he is).

These questions and others related to them are beyond the scope of **syntax**, beyond the scope of anything that we can systematize or standardize as parts of linguistics or levels of analysis that linguistics can handle. Obviously these questions are related to meaning, but they are beyond the features and dimensions of meaning that are integrated into linguistics under the heading of **semantics**. Such questions are examined in linguistics under the heading of *pragmatics*—knowledge about the relation between what is said and what in the world it refers to. But we are getting ahead of our story.

A Punctuation Path in the
Semantic Forest of Syntactic Trees

What a difference the dots make to the right connections. Here are two dear John letters with identical words but worlds apart. (From *Games Magazine*, 1984)

> Dear John,
> I want a man who knows what love is all about. You are generous, kind, thoughtful. People who are not like you admit to being useless and inferior. You have ruined me for other men. I yearn for you. I have no feelings whatsoever when we are apart. I can be forever happy. Will you let me be yours? Gloria.

> Dear John,
> I want a man who knows what love is. All about you are generous, kind, thoughtful people, who are not like you. Admit to being useless and inferior. You have ruined me. For other men, I yearn. For you, I have no feelings whatsoever. When we are apart, I can be forever happy. Will you let me be? Yours, Gloria.

A Middle Ground

For purposes of describing language fully and accurately, linguistics isolates functional units of language at the levels of analysis we have identified so far: **phonology**, *morphology*, **syntax**, and **semantics**. It is important not to oversharpen the distinction among these, important to understand that when language is in action, units from different levels come into play together. Here are examples of (1) *he* and *him* playing tag as a new sentence pattern develops in English (*morphology* and **syntax** interact); (2) two senseless sentences, where one shows itself to be superior (**syntax** and **semantics** interact).

(1) "Him was given a book:" How Now, Noam Chomsky?

Most people would agree that there is something wrong with saying "Him was given a book." We should say "He was given a book." Instead of making this kind of judgment and imposing a rule of usage, the linguist confines herself to describing language. A full linguistic description of English includes the changes in the language that have taken place since the days when speakers *did* say "Him was given a book."

Clearly our sentence means that the book was given *to him*, and not that he did something (it's the basic job of subject pronouns such as *he* to indicate who performs an action). "He was given a book" is less logical than "Him was given a book," with its use of an object pronoun (it's the basic job of an object pronoun to indicate who is on the receiving end of an action, whether it be a punch in the nose or the gift of a book). But we don't much like "him" up front in the sentence, because it doesn't follow the pattern of sentences we use much more often starting with "he was" (followed by any verb). The "He was..." pattern created a pressure that caused sentences of the type "Him was given a book" to disappear.

These are the facts of the case described from a linguist's point of view, and they show why linguistics avoids passing judgment on language use: what was "wrong" once upon a time ("He was given a book") is now "right" and what was at that time "right" ("Him was given a book") is now "wrong."

(2) And Chomsky in his Green Period

One of the best known and often quoted examples discussed in the early writings of Chomsky is the sentence "Colorless green ideas sleep furiously." His point in discussing this sentence was to show that what makes a sentence grammatically well formed is not predictable on semantic grounds alone. "Colorless green ideas sleep furiously" has pretty good **syntax**, even though semantically it is a mess. It shares a tree structure with "Serious university students work diligently," and that makes it superior syntactically to "Furiously sleep ideas green color-

less," even though both are meaningless. So this example may seem to give a reason for keeping **semantics** out of **syntax**, but we have seen enough other examples already to understand that **syntax** and **semantics** are fundamentally (and functionally) inseparable.

How Many Languages Can Fit on a Planet?

Let's take a little break from looking at how linguists do their studies and look instead at what they study: languages worldwide. Nobody knows for sure how many languages there are, though we do know that their number is diminishing. (Since 1928, linguists have been holding an international congress every five years, and the theme of the 1992 congress in Quebec city, Canada, was endangered languages). Estimates range from under 3000 to over 5000.

It is rare for a language to have no known relatives, but Basque, spoken in the Pyrenees Mountains straddling France and Spain, is perhaps the best-known case.

Others include Ainu (Japan), Burushaski (India), and Ket (Siberia).

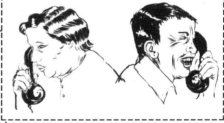

Most languages come in families that range dramatically in size. The Romance languages, derived from Latin, number 13 today (the lesser known members of the family include Galician, Romansch, Ladin, Friulian, and Aromunian), but the Bantu group, spoken in central and southern Africa, runs to over five hundred languages and dialects. Vast as it is, the Bantu family belongs to an even larger group known as the Niger-Congo languages.

Austronesian is a group of no less than 1,000 languages whose speakers are to be found from Madagascar to New Zealand. So there is no shortage of work for linguists who are prepared to trek off and do field work recording the incredibly rich variety of languages in our world.

There are more than twenty families of native languages in the Americas, known collectively as the Amerind languages. But language families spill over geographic boundaries: the Afroasiatic languages, as their name indicates, span Africa and Asia, and likewise the members of the vast Indo-European group stretch from the northernmost regions of Europe to the Indian subcontinent.

If there is no single answer to the question we started with (How many languages can fit on a planet?), we do at least have an idea of what the squeeze-rate is here on earth: in Papua, New Guinea, with an area only slightly larger than California and a population of just

over three million, there are nearly 900 separate languages.
We've been talking here about natural languages, but linguists started inventing artificial languages long ago, in the hope of making international communication easier. Esperanto is one of the best known. It blends elements from existing widely spoken language in a noble and democratic effort to allow the peoples of the world to communicate in a common language. But this approach has not always been the starting point for linguistic internationalism...

Nuclear English/Basic English

Nuclear English is not English for the atomic age but a proposed core language derived from full English (compare *Basic English*) and intended as an international medium of communication. What a difference a capital letter makes. Basic English is basic, but it is not simply basic English. A carefully worked out system, consisting of 850 words and the rules for their use, Basic English was developed by British scholar Charles Kay Ogden (1889-1957) as an international auxiliary language. Ogden believed it would help promote world peace. Basic is an acronym for British, American, Scientific, International, Commercial. The champions of Basic English included such masters of language as Winston Churchill, Lawrence Durrell, and Ezra Pound. Critics dismissed it, charging that it turned a sentence from standard English such as "The officer led his soldiers against the enemy, but the enemy stood firm" into a clumsy clunker: "The person in military authority was the guide of his men in the army against the nation at war, but the not-friends stood solidly upright." This version, conveniently awkward for detractors, violates the rules of the Basic system; if they are respected, it comes out rather well: "The lieutenant went in front of his men to the attack, but the other side did not give way."

We'll be looking at more of the languages of the world a little later on. In the meantime, it's back to some basics about how language works.

What's the Buzz?

What do bees, computers, and traffic signals have in common? They get messages across, in ways that are both similar and different from each other. And especially different from the human languages that linguists study and analyze.

A surge of electrical current through bulbs under red, green, and amber glass tells us to stop, go, or be careful.

The lights give their messages *to* us, but they *do* not communicate *with* us. (They don't much care if we get the message, they don't expect us to reply, and they wouldn't understand us if we did.)

Bees give us a definite message if they choose to sting us, but for the most part they exchange information about how far away a source of nectar is and how to get there. Pretty sophisticated stuff compared to *stop* and *go*, and it is expressed in a code of micrometrically controlled gestures (often referred to as a "dance") that leaves the traffic lights back at the corner. Even so, the point of the bees' bulletin board body language is not much different from that of the traffic signals—posting instructions.

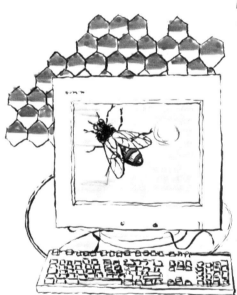

Now computers seem to beat the bees for sophistication, but that is an illusion created by the power of the computer to *display* data in an infinite variety of forms. No matter how complex the data our pentium pet may be handling, it all reduces to yes or no, plus or minus, one or zero, galaxies of ones and zeros, down in those

solid-state gizzards that we don't see and don't usually think about. And the software "languages" that run those circuits at our pleasure are strings of commands, basically no different from the stop and go of traffic lights.

What makes human languages so fundamentally different from computer languages, from the DOS of the bee drive, or from that tricolored winker at the intersection, is *meaning*, in all the complexity that our minds can give it. From the features of language that we have already had a look at and the parts of linguistics that we have defined so far, we can put together a definition of language that will lead us to the next level of analysis:

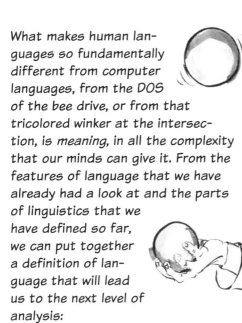

HUMAN LANGUAGE IS A CLOSED SET OF SOUNDS AND A LIMITED SET OF RULES....

...FOR MAKING AND SHARING MEANINGS.

There are a few things we would need to add to this definition to make it as complete as possible, for example that the only place a specific language exists in its fullest form is in the memory of members of a speech community. And of course while the ideas behind words like *set* and *sound* and *rules* are clear enough from our general knowledge, the meaning of *meaning* is pretty slippery. As it happens, *The Meaning of Meaning* is the name of a book that has been in print continuously since 1923, and it will be our starting point for looking at **semantics**.

Semantics *(also called "Meaning")*

The Meaning of Meaning is by two dead white males who gave the world this, their first book, when they were roughly the same tender age as the Chomsky of *Syntactic Structures*. (Linguistics has

always been a field for young persons.) Charles Kay Ogden (1889–1957) and Ivor Armstrong Richards (1893–1979), who met as students at Cambridge University, were appalled at what a hash linguists and philosophers alike were making of the study of meaning.

SEMANTICS study of meaning

They set about cleaning up the mess by placing themselves at the crossroads where linguistics meets psychology, philosophy, and anthropology (linguistics as a whole displays this interdisciplinary nature more than ever today). For good measure, they also chose the meeting point of linguistics and *semiotics*.

Psychology

Philosophy

Anthropology

This is the general study of signs, i.e., of anything that stands for something other than itself, a

SEMIOTICS study of signs

MEANING OF MEANING

study extending beyond the scope of verbal language. Ogden and Richards anchored much of their book in the work of the amazing American thinker and founder of modern semiotics, Charles Sanders Peirce (1839–1914).

For Ogden and Richards, the shabby analysis of language in their day redeemed itself through Peirce, whose work on semiotics first became widely available through an appendix they published in *The Meaning of Meaning*. In the definition of the sign at the base of Peirce's work one discovers the most far-reaching influence on Ogden and Richards. Ogden later pointed out that logic for Peirce

> In the definition of the sign at the base of Peirce's work, one discovers the most far reaching influence on Ogden and Richards.

was the equivalent of the general theory of signs. In this respect there is also a parallel with *The Meaning of Meaning*, because the rules the authors propose for keeping meaning under control are a reworked version of philosophy's traditional rules of logic.

Ogden and Richards are critical of Saussure for rejecting the term *symbol* to designate the linguistic sign. Saussure reserves *symbol* for a limited group of signs that he defines very carefully, but this is not good enough for Ogden and Richards. They see Saussure's distinction between sign and symbol as irrelevant and substitute their own: symbols communicate by putting signs into sign-situations. On this view, all symbols are signs; not all signs are symbols. So Ogden & Richards set up a relationship between sign and symbol on the basis of *function*, whereas Saussure keeps them apart on the basis of their relative *qualities*.

The Meaning of Meaning is much too long for us to give a full sum-
mary of it here, so we will look at only two more points about it.

Word Magic

Ogden and Richards use this phrase
to describe thought under the control
of language instead of language under
the control of thought. Much of
Ogden's later work, especially the 850-
word system of Basic English he developed (see below under *Universal
Language*) were part of a program for
eradicating word magic. Word magic is
at the heart of taboos on the use of
language (such as saying *goldarn* to
avoid saying *God damn*) and beliefs
about the power of language revealed in
clichés such as *speak of the devil*, with its
suggestion that the word *devil*, and words
in general, are so powerful that they can
conjure up the things they stand for.

The Phonetic Subterfuge

The Meaning of Meaning is a rich and
erudite book. It is also written in
smart-alecky, stay-with-me-if-you-are-
smart-enough style and pokes fun at
cumbersome terminology in linguistics
(the kind we are trying hard to keep out
of this book). This is what the authors are doing when they come up
with a series of phrases that starts with **phonetic** subterfuge. If we
imagine that a word follows the pattern of meaning

of other words just
because it sounds similar,
Ogden and Richards declare,
we are guilty of the **phonetic** subterfuge. An example?
(Ours, not theirs:) "Leasable"
means available for lease;
"loanable" means available for
loan; "lovable" does not mean
available for love.

Some of Ogden's and Richards's whimsy has baffled even the most erudite of readers, including polymath Douglas Hofstadter, the author of *Metamagical Themas*, *Le ton beau de Marot*, and *Gödel, Escher, Bach*. Nevertheless, the book inspired Hofstadter to pen these lines:

> Two experts, to explicate Meaning,
> Penned a text called "The Meaning of Meaning,"
> But the world was perplexed,
> So three experts penned next
> "The Meaning of Meaning of Meaning."

Not to Put too Fine a Point on It

But even those who walk away from *The Meaning of Meaning* scratching their heads remember its three main points:

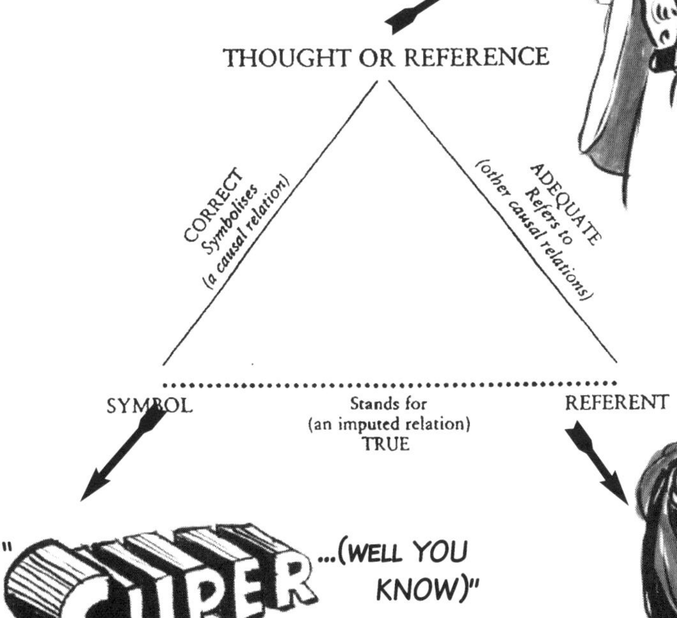

THOUGHT OR REFERENCE

CORRECT
Symbolises
(a causal relation)

ADEQUATE
Refers to
(other causal relations)

SYMBOL

Stands for
(an imputed relation)
TRUE

REFERENT

"SUPER ...(WELL YOU KNOW)"

Few scholars have appreciated that, far from being a mere visual convenience to readers, the triangle unifies the ideas developed in *The Meaning of Meaning*. (It is also another link from Ogden and Richards to Peirce.)

But why a triangle diagram? Because its three points are the indispensable ingredients of meaning. Four are not required and two are not enough.

Symbol = word, phrase, sentence (SUPER...); *referent* = what in the world the symbol stands for ( ); *thought* = 1) what referent the symbol makes us think of when we hear or read a message; 2) what symbol the referent makes us think of when we want to tell the world about it ( ). If we take away any one of these, there is no communication.

There are many ways to define meaning and many approaches to the study of meaning. If we focus on words, we can look at them individually (especially those that have complex meanings), in pairs (especially those that have similar or opposite meanings), or in groups (especially those that share meanings). Or we can study how these various states of meaning came about.

Multiple Meanings

Many words have more than one meaning. This is normal. The more a word is used, the more it occurs in new contexts, and the more chance it has of acquiring new meaning(s) from those contexts. An extreme case in English is the word *set*, with 128 meanings listed in the *Oxford English Dictionary*.

Homonyms...

remember?

NOAM

gnome

...are words

that sound the same (though they are not necessarily spelled the same way) but have different meanings. Homonyms can lead to confusion, even among persons who know a lot about their language.

Here is an example:

There are versions of the Cinderella story in many languages around the world. The one commonly told in English came via France, where Charles Perrault (1628-1703) recorded in writing the stories told to his children by their Basque nurse. The *glass slipper* figures in Perrault's version, and corresponds to the crystal slipper of the Scots-Irish and other versions of Cinderella. Well and good, but not good enough two centuries later for two distinguished French *literati*, Honoré de Balzac and Emile Littré, who assumed that a confusion had arisen because the French words for *glass* (*verre*) and for *squirrel fur* (*vair*) are pronounced the same. Surely a fur slipper makes more sense than a glass slipper. Maybe, but this is a story. And it's a crystal or glass slipper even in languages where the words for *glass* and *fur* are *not* pronounced the same way and where no confusion could have occurred. How now, messieurs Balzac et Littré?

[49

How Many Meanings?

A fight broke out in a kitchen. Egged on by the waiters, two cooks peppered each other with punches. One man, a greasy foie gras specialist, ducked the first blows, but his goose was cooked. The man who beet him, a salad expert with big cauliflower ears, tried to flee the scene but was cornered in the maize of tables by a husky off-duty cob. He was charged with a salt and battery. He claims to be looking forward to the suit, because he has always wanted to be a sous-chef.

Change of Meaning

In Old English, *sam*, the equivalent of Latin *semi-*, meant "half." *Sand-blind*, attested in the fifteenth century, is likely a variant of *samblind*—"half-blind." The prefix was already well on its way to being associated only with *sand* when Shakespeare wrote in *The Merchant of Venice*: "This is my true begotten father, who being more than sand-blinde, high gravel blinde, knows me not." And that pillar of erudition, Samuel Johnson, defined *sand-blind* in *A Dictionary of the English Language* (1755) as "having a defect in the eyes, by which small particles appear to fly before them." Our cited phrase comes from the poetry of Walter de la Mare: "Hope...Led sand-blind Despair To a clear babbling well-spring And laved his eyes there."

Synonyms...

...are words that share meaning. It is a lot less common to find two or more words with exactly the same meaning. And the question of style comes into the picture. A poem titled "The Death of Roget" by George Hatch, Jr., gives a whimsical account of the fate of Peter Mark Roget, the man who gave the world its best-known dictionary of synonyms:

Said Roget:
 "What's the purpose? Tell me why.
 What's the reason? Specify!
The other was silent,
speechless, mum,
close-mouthed, firm-tongued,
tight-lipped and dumb,
word-bound, curt, concise and brief:
He drew a gun, a gat, a rod,
and waved it in Roget's façade,
his face, his mug,
his map, his lug,
his kisser.
"Now wait a minute!" cried Roget.
"Wait a second! Stop! Delay—!"
That's all he said, the other fired,
shot him once; Roget expired,
pegged out, conked out,
kicked the bucket,
croaked and piped. With
Roget's luck it
means he's dead, defunct, passed on,
deceased, demised, lamented, gone.
They wrapped him up in polished oak,
a coffin, casket, wooden cloak,
and on his grave these words bespoke:
"Lie in peace; to God bequest...
 R.I.P. and all the rest..."

Semantic Accidents

In our last four sections, we isolated and defined features of language, illustrating them with various words, word pairs, and word groups. These same features of language can come together in a single example, as in the case of the phrase *piggy bank*. This happens by chance and produces some interesting results.

Once upon a time, there was a good old English word *pygg*, meaning a type of material much like earthenware. Containers made out of pygg were called *pyggs*. So far, no surprises. After all, a container made out of glass is called a *glass*, one made out of tin is called a *tin*, etc. A pygg used for storing coins was called a *penny-pig, pence-pig*, etc. When pygg went the way of ceramic hammers, speakers of English soon forgot what the *pygg* part of *penny-pig* meant and made a new connection instead with *pig*. As a result, coin banks began to be fashioned in the shape of the animal. So the chain of events here takes us from the development of a new meaning for *pygg* (container) through loss of meaning (no more *pygg* as material) and homonyms (*pygg/pig*) to the modern *piggy bank*. At this last stage, there seems to be an obvious reason for the thing to be called *piggy bank*, but if we know the history of the word, this turns out to be pure fiction.

A Flurry of Words for Snow

Even without having read one word about linguistics before, you probably have a vague idea that there are "a lot of Eskimo words for snow." When we look closely at the data, we discover that one part misinformation has been mixed with ten parts of exaggeration to produce some bootleg linguistics here. A real snow job.

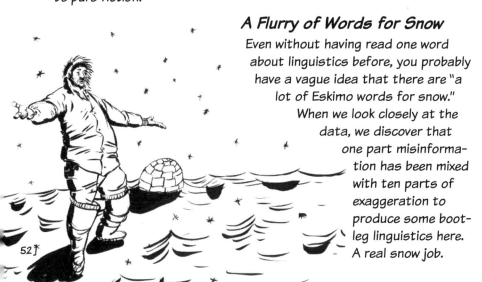

It all started quite innocently when the grandfather of American linguistics, anthropologist Franz Boas (1858-1942), pointed out that just as different words in English express different forms of water (*lake, river, brook, etc.*), so too "Eskimo" [we're going to explain the reason for the quotation marks two paragraphs from now, so we'll stop using them in the meantime] has a variety of terms: *aput* 'snow on the ground', *gana* 'falling snow', *piqsirpoq* 'drifting snow', and *qimuqsuq* 'a snow drift'.

Boas's point was that English gets these ideas across with phrases using the single term *snow*, though it could have evolved a variety of forms, as it did for *lake, river, brook, etc.* In other words, when we look back to the original comment by Boas, we discover that he is pointing out not a contrast but a similarity between how language can and does work in the case of English and Eskimo.

hmm...
4 Eskimo terms
× 7 phrases
= 400 words
for snow!

Benjamin Whorf

Boas's discussion made its way into the writings of linguist Benjamin Lee Whorf (1897-1941), who turned the four Eskimo terms cited by Boas (Did he know of others? If so, he didn't say.) into seven phrases about snow in English, implying that there could be any number of additional ones in Eskimo! The beast was loose. In the meantime, there have been "reports" of up to 400 Eskimo words for snow!

If Boas were alive today, he might well ask what are the 396 that mysteriously got added to his examples. He would certainly shake his head at the shabby brand of linguistics that refers to a non-existent, generic "Eskimo" language and at the failure to make the distinction between *words* as such and *roots* from which any num-

But there is NO "ESKIMO" language!

FRANZ BOAS

ber of words (about snow or ice or just about anything else) can be formed in languages such as Labradorian Inuit and West Greenlandic. Here are some examples and their English equivalents:

Labradorian Inuit
****

pukak – granular snow
masak – soft snow
mauja – soft, deep snow
mangokpak – watery snow
massalerauvok – snow filled with water

West Greenlandic
****

sullarniq – snow blown in (to doorway, etc.)
nittaalaq – air thick with snow
qanipalaat – feathery clumps of falling snow
apusiniq – snowdrift
imalik – wet snow falling

A total of 49 words for types of snow and
ice in West Greenlandic is given on the website
www.urbanlegends.com.

How Many Linguists Does it Take to Change a Lightbulb?

Eight. A semanticist to write a paper on the meaning of "a lightbulb,"
a semiologist to write a paper on the meaning of a lightbulb, a journal editor to point out that, following Saussure, not everyone would
agree that a semiologist is a kind of linguist, a Chomskyan to set
the switch to on or off, a Neogrammarian to reconstruct the dead
bulb from all the burnt out ones, a proponent of interlanguage to
analyze the complex transfer phenomena before attempting a
changeover, a discourse analyst to record, transcribe, and analyze
the work of the other linguists, as they argue in the dark, and a
pragmaticist to find the right words to persuade the janitor to
change the bulb right away.

The Best Meaning Is the Least Meaning

This statement may seem like an odd way to end our look at **semantics**, but it is nothing more than a lesson on the importance of getting meaning from context. It is a way of saying that if we do not know the exact meaning of a word when we hear or read it in a specific context, it is safest to choose among the possible meanings by taking the one that makes the word least different from the meaning already set up by that context. To illustrate the point, let's take as an example a sentence where we *do* know the meaning of the final word, where that meaning is *so* obvious that we would not normally bother to check for the other possible meanings:

> The rider dug in his spurs to urge on his mount.

There is enough coherent information in the sentence before we get to *mount* to tell us that it is being used in the sense of *horse*. We eliminate the meanings i) object used to display another; ii) object used for support; iii) hill or mountain. We even eliminate meanings more closely related to the context (act of mounting, style of mounting) virtually without thinking about them.

The best-meaning-as-least-meaning rule simply reminds us that the way we process meanings more or less automatically when confronted with known words is the same way we should proceed when a word puzzles us.

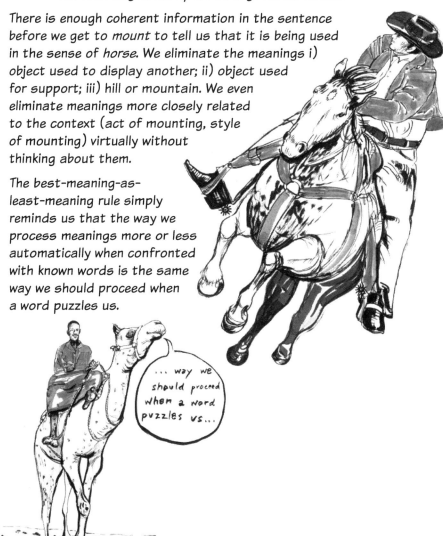

... way we should proceed when a word puzzles us...

By Way of Review (but no quiz)

Look at the two sentences following. What is special about them? What have you learned about linguistics so far that can help you describe them?

He's none too wise, replies the old man, muttering.
He's known two wise replies, the old man muttering.

Answer (we're not even going to bother turning it upside down at the bottom of the page):

1) The sentences are different by only one **phoneme** (the vowel in *none* and *known*);
2) They contain the homonyms *too* and *two*;
3) They have very different meanings because of 1) and 2) *and because they have different tree structures.*
4) The different meanings for the two sentences can be recognized in part by the contrast in intonation (rise and fall of the voice) between them.

A FEW FINAL LESSONS ON HOW LANGUAGES WORK

From Tones and Whistles to Clicks and Klingon and the Case of Case

In our warp-speed survey of linguistics we have had to leave out a lot of interesting facts about how different languages work and the challenges that linguists face in analyzing them. Here are a few to help us fill in the picture.

(1) Name that Tone

Cantonese, Hausa (Nigeria/Cameroun), Mandarin, Margi (Nigeria), Thai, and Yoruba (Nigeria/Benin). Like more than 50% of the world's languages, each of these is what is known as a tonal language, where the tones (changes in pitch) make a difference in meaning. Say "Ma" with a high and level tone in English and you are calling your mother; say it with a high and falling tone and you are letting her know you are exasperated with her, but she's still your mother. In Mandarin, make

[57

the same switch and the meaning of the syllable "ma" goes from "mother" to "scold."

All tonal languages have at least two tones, and there are some with eight or more, but these are rare. Differences in meaning between the same sylla- ble in two dif- ferent tones are not always as radical as in our Mandarin example. In Nigeria's Kanuri language, for example, tone distinguishes among the tenses of a verb.

In writing, tones can only be shown by symbols that differ from each other, even though the sounds they represent are the same, as hap- pens with our two *mas* in Mandarin (and two more that mean "hemp" and "horse"). But they can make it onto the airwaves by other means than the human voice, as in the case of African "talking drums" that reproduce the rhythms and tones of speech.

(2) Colonel Bogey Would Have Loved It

These same rhythms and tones, detached from the syllables that they normally belong to, can be whistled by speakers. The patterns formed by the rhythms and tones are distinctive enough even without specific speech sounds to make communication possible. The whistled message is interpreted by filling in the missing sounds. As long as you and the person you are conversing with stay in key, there will be no confusion over "ball" and "small", etc.

Mini-Review

Do *ball* and *small* make a minimal pair? Look back to our section on **phonology**. The answer is "no," because they differ by more than one sound. What about *ball* and *mall* or *ball* and *all*? "Yes" to both, because the difference in meaning in each pair depends on a difference of just one sound.

There are no whistled languages, no communication systems consisting *entirely* of whistles, only whistled versions of tonal languages. Whistling is an option here.

(3) Click Here, Click There

Clicking is not an option in the Khoisan languages of southern Africa. Practically the only clicking sound we make or recognize as speakers of English is the one usually written *tsk, tsk*—a signal of disapproval. It is a full-fledged click, produced by pulling the tongue away from the upper teeth. A distinctive sound results when the mouth is suddenly unblocked by the movement of the tongue and air enters.

Variations on this process are at work in all the languages of the Khoisan family, where the difference in pronunciation between various clicks makes just as much difference to meaning as /p/, /t/, and /m/ do in *pan, tan,* and *man*. Clicks can occur at just about every point of articulation in the mouth and can even accompany other sounds produced in the throat or the nasal cavity, making for a huge number of possibilities. The !Xu language has 48 different varieties of clicks—in addition to 47 other non-click consonants! We are a long way from *tsk, tsk,* but not as far away as the speakers of Klingon...

(4) No Clicks in Klingon

...those aliens in *Star Trek*. Paramount Pictures wanted a harsh and guttural language for them, and Washington linguist Marc Okrand provided it. Though there is more of cult than culture surrounding Klingon, the non-profit Klingon Language Institute describes its chief aim as being the facilitation of scholarly exploration of the language *and* its culture. Written Klingon (a translation of Hamlet is available) uses the English alphabet but breaks with its conventions by using capitals wherever required in a word as reminders that the pronunciation of a letter differs from that of English. A beginner's guide warns that confusing q and Q in Klingon is as serious as confusing /f/ and /g/ in English.

£	⍦	⍣	⍢	⌐	⊥	ρ
a	b	ch	D	e	gh	H
⍦	⍲	⌐	ρ	€	⌐	⌐
I	j	l	m	n	ng	o
⌐	⌐	⌐	⊁	⌐	⌐	⌐
P	q	Q	r	S	t	tlh
⌐	⌐	⌐	◀	⌐		
u	v	w	y	'		
—	⌐	⟨	⌐	⌐	⌐	⌐
0	1	2	3	4	5	6
⌐	✖	⬆				
7	8	9				

KLINGON FUN!

Klingon's *gh* is not the *gh* of *rough, through,* or any other English word but a gargled sound something like a French /r/. The absence of clicks probably does not make Klingon any easier to pronounce than !Xu. *q,* for example, must be pronounced as far back in the mouth as possible with the back of the tongue touching the uvula. It is related to *Q,* the difference being that the first sounds a little like you are choking and the second sounds a lot like you are choking. If you don't find this too intimidating or discouraging, you could soon join the legions having fun with Klingon or practice the linguistic skills you are acquiring here by analysing the language.

(5) Case

This has to do with the way in which the connections among words are expressed. In English we make many such connections by using words belonging to the category known as *prepositions (of, by, with, in, from, etc.)*. In other languages (called *inflected languages*), it is not separate words that get these ideas across but changes in the basic form of a word. Here are some examples from Basque:

etxearen – of the house
etxeaz – by means of the house
etxearekin – with the house
etxean – in the house
etxetik – from/out of the house

ETXEAREN

ETXEAZ

Etxearekin

ETXETIK

LANGUAGES IN CONTACT

We Talk Tok Pisin Here, They Talk Tolaki There...

It's not a joke. *Tok Pisin* is the name of a language. The name comes from *talk pidgin.*

(When the speakers of two or more languages in contact work out a common means of communication with a limited number of words from their languages and very simple grammatical rules, the product is called *pidgin.*) Tok Pisin, based on English and in use since the end of the nineteenth century, is spoken by over two million people as a second language in Papua, New Guinea. The older name for Tok Pisin is Melanesian Pidgin English. Here are some samples of Tok Pisin.

Let's start with one word:

yumitupela

It was four words in English: you+me+two+people. This is the pronoun *we,* when *we* refers only to the person speaking and the person being spoken to.

Now full sentences:

Bandarap em i kukim (Bandarap cooked it).

Meri hilans i karamapim het wantaim bilas
(Women from the highlands cover their heads with decorations).

You can check out the daily news in Tok Pisin from the Radio Australia home page.

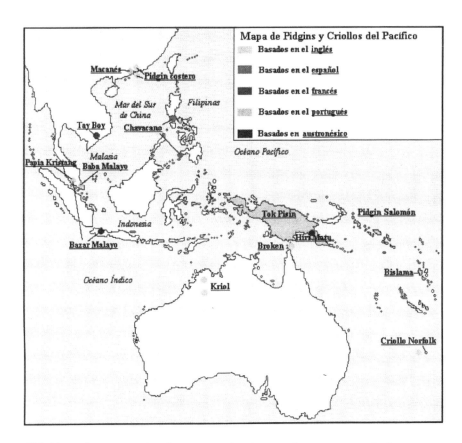

Tolaki, an Austronesian language, is the mother tongue of about 125,000 speakers in south-eastern Sulawesi. Here's a small start on learning the very distinctive names of some of the languages on space-ship Earth:

Bobo Fing - a Niger-Congo language of Burkina Faso and Mali

Lü - Known by three other names, Lü is variety of the Tai Yuan language of Northern Thailan. It is a tonal language (see below) spoken in Yunnan.

Gutnius

Jon i raitim

1 [1] Bipo bipo tru, taim olgeta samting i no kamap yet, Tok i stap. Tok i stap wantaim God na Tok em yet i God. [2] Bipo bipo tru Tok i stap wantaim God. [3] Long dispela Tok tasol God i mekim kamap olgeta samting. Na i no gat wanpela samting i kamap long narapela rot. Nogat. Olgeta samting i kamap, em Tok yet i mekim kamap. [4] Laip i stap long em, na dispela laip em i lait bilong ol manmeri. [5] Dispela lait i save lait i stap long tudak, na tudak i no bin daunim em.

[6] Wanpela man i kamap, nem bilong en Jon. God i bin salim em i kam. [7] Em i kam bilong autim tok. Em i autim tok bilong dispela lait, bai olgeta manmeri i ken harim tok bilong em, na ol i ken bilip. [8] Em yet em i no dispela lait. Nogat. Em i kam bilong autim tok tasol bilong dispela lait. [9] Dispela lait em i lait tru na i save givim lait long olgeta manmeri, em i laik i kam long graun.

Zaza – This is an Iranian language, quite distinct from Kurdish, spoken by perhaps two million persons in Iran and Turkey.

Bishnupriya Manipuru – It is a little easier to remember by its other name: Mayang. This is a form of Bengali (an Indo-Aryan language with 180 million speakers today in Bangladesh and India). Mayang is spoken in three regions of Bangladesh.

Fox – a member of the huge Algonquian family of aboriginal languages of North America

Kickapoo – a member of the huge Algonquian family of aboriginal languages of North America

Hyperborean – The word referred in classical Greek to a mythical people who lived "beyond the North Wind" (this is the direct translation of *Hyperborean*). In linguistics, this is the older name for *Palaeosiberian* (meaning "old Siberian") – minority languages of Siberia that are unrelated to other languages.

Loka of Mustang - also known as *Kagate*, a Tibetan dialect spoken by the Sherpa and their kin in Nepal

Romblomanon - an Austronesian language with 200,000 speakers in the Romblon and Sibuyan Islands

Sre - an Austroasiatic language

Here are a few more names of languages, some with echoes of those above, but one purely fictitious. Guess which?

Bobo Wule, Li, Hre, Roratongan, Zezuru, Kimbundu, Coeur d'Alène, Lokko, Iron, Huihui, Binkoka, Yi.

Did you guess the one that seems to stick out the most, *Coeur d'Alène* (French for "Alène's heart")? This is the name of a language in the Salish family of North American aboriginal languages. (It's also the name of a town in the great American state of Idaho.) All the others are genuine too, except Binkoka, though it has an echo suggestive of *Bingkokak*, an Austronesian language.

Creoles

A creole is a language descended from a *pidgin* (look back to our Tok Pisin section). In some cases, a pidgin becomes so well established in a multilingual society that a generation of speakers grows up using only the pidgin to communicate among themselves. When this happens, the vocabulary of the pidgin expands and a full grammatical system develops, promoting the former pidgin to the status of a complete language system. This type of new language, when it develops spontaneously, is called a *creole*. The transformation of a pidgin into a creole is called *creolization*. (English and African tongues blended to form the Gullah creole spoken on a narrow coastal strip of South Carolina, Georgia, and northeastern Florida.)

Lingua franca

This is the name given to a language used over a large area where people speak a variety of languages. The term originally meant 'Frankish language,' i.e., the language of the Franks, the ancient Germanic tribe that lived on the banks of the Rhine in the early Christian era. (The Salian Franks gave their name to France when they conquered Gaul in the 5th century.) During the late medieval period, the lingua franca used for commerce in the eastern Mediterranean was an Italian dialect mixed with French, Spanish, Greek, Arabic and Turkish. The term is used to refer to any language adopted as a means of communication by speakers of different languages who inhabit the same region. In its broadest sense, *lingua franca* refers to *pidgins*

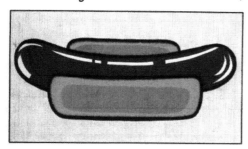

and/or *creoles*, though most linguists would reject this usage as too loose to be a reflection of linguistic facts as we have described them here.

Probably the most generally accepted use of *lingua franca* among linguists at present would be as the term for a well-established language whose native speakers have the status of a prestige group, as a consequence of which the language comes into use for communication among groups of speakers of various other languages. This is the case for Swahili in East Africa, Hausa in West Africa, and English in Singapore and elsewhere.

Languages as Life rafts

Two translators are talking shop aboard a ship when it suddenly begins to sink:
"Can you swim?" asks one.
"No," replies the other, "but I can shout for help in nine languages."

HOW HUMANS LEARN THEIR LANGUAGES

The Linguist Within

An idea that Noam Chomsky and other linguists have promoted in recent years is that we are born hard-wired to learn language. The jury is still out on this question, but we know for sure that children acquire the complexities of language with amazing speed and facility. This happens in a way that is marked by such a high degree of organization, that it gives weight to Chomsky's claim. So what does the **syntax** of an eighteen-month old linguist look like?

Basically, it's a set of rules that let tiny tykes put words together to express relationships— the same relationships that show up later when the little gaffers get full control of language— such as topic and modifier, verb and object, sub-

ject and predicate. And just like full-blown **syntax**, the toddler's scaled-down model excludes certain combinations. This has nothing to do with "bad grammar" (who could understand such a concept when they are still in diapers?) but

everything to do with imposing limits and restrictions that make the child's emerging grasp of language (and the world that language is about) coherent and systematic.

Single words are used as full sentences when infants begin to speak (the word *infant* comes to us from Greek and means "not speaking"). Our linguist taking first steps across the living room floor and into the wide and wonderful world of language may know both "bye-bye" and "daddy"

but will not use the words together.

When, at around 18 months of age, the child does launch into two-word phrases, her entire vocabulary falls into two groups. The larger one consists of words that can stand by themselves to form a message (shoe, hot, milk), but words from the smaller second group are never used alone (my, green). Instead, they occur in combination with a word from the first group. The full set of rules for a generative **syntax** of the sentences of eighteenth-month old speakers can be summarized as follows, where S stands for a sentence, I for potentially independent words, R for words restricted to combinations, and the linguist's arrow has the same function as the mathematician's equal sign (=).

$$S \longrightarrow I$$
$$S \longrightarrow I + I$$
$$S \longrightarrow I + R$$
$$S \longrightarrow R + I$$

So, of all sentence types that could occur, two do not, namely S ——> R and S ——> R + R. This is not a theory. This is about what young speakers do and do not say: "Milk hot," "Green ball," "Daddy gone," "My sock" but never "Green my" or "My green" or "My" or "Green". Most children learn to make 3-word sentences by their second birthday. These sentences too show patterns that *prohibit* certain combinations. Generative **syntax**, as Chomsky pointed out long ago, is very powerful, too powerful even at the simple sentence stage, because not all possible 3-word combinations are used. The rules that generate even the first 3-word sentences found in child speech are basically the same in form as those used in the description of adult language in all its complexity. It seems that children begin to get a handle on language by recognizing different relationships among words. When this knowledge is mastered, they proceed to learn transformational rules and procedures for creating the fully-formed structures of their language community in all acceptable varieties.

Baby Wants...Leche?

A childless Canadian couple decided to adopt a Mexican baby. As soon as they got the child, they enrolled in a Spanish course. When asked why, they replied, "so that when the baby starts to talk, we'll be able to understand him."

THE BIRTH OF LANGUAGE,
THE GROWTH AND DEATH OF LANGUAGES

Word One

Humans are naturally curious about how language began. We might ask: what was the first word ever spoken? It's an interesting question, but from the linguist's point of view, not a very good one,

because it makes an assumption that is not true. If there is a word, it has to belong to a language system. The first utterance could not have been a word, because there was no system in place yet for it belong to. Language developed over a very long time before anybody ever wrote down anything about anything, much less about language itself, so the answer to our questions about the origins of language are lost forever in the mists of time. This has not stopped speculation, and at least five main theories have emerged. We give them here under the popular names by which they are known.

The Bow-Wow Theory

Spoken language began with human beings imitating sounds in the natural environment, particularly animal calls.

The Pooh-Pooh Theory

Spoken language started with humans producing sounds instinctively in response to pain, anger, and other bodily troubles.

The Ding-Dong Theory

The roots of language are to be found in spontaneous human reaction to stimuli in the environment, taking the form of sounds which mirror or harmonize with that environment. (This is the Bow-Wow Theory making the move from the kennel to the cosmos.)

The Yo-Heave-Ho Theory

The origins of speech can be traced to communal, physical labour, the exertion required producing rhythmical grunts that developed first into chants and eventually into full-fledged language.

The La-La Theory

This is the contribution of the romantically inclined to explaining the beginnings of human language: it all stemmed from sounds associated with love, the irrepressible joy of the human spirit, the expression of poetic feeling, the sublimity of the song of the heart that must out.

Language Change

Change in language is inevitable with the passing of time. Languages change constantly. Words are added to the vocabulary, some disappear, and the meanings of others shift and grow. Pronunciations, grammatical forms, and sentence structures change too. As long as a language remains in use, change cannot be avoided.

The why of language change is complex and varied: new inventions, new concepts, and new activities bring in new words; words may acquire or lose social prestige according to circumstances and become more widespread or rarer as a result; grammatical structures may be simplified as a result of high frequency of use; and contact among speakers of different languages may lead to the borrowing of forms and usages from one linguistic community or the other.

The result of never-ending language change is a steady increase in the divergence between a language at any stage in its development and the form of the language from which it derived. And to complicate the picture, a language spoken over a wide area undergoes changes at different rates in different places. The result, over a long stretch of time, is a break up. At first, distinct regional *dialects* emerge; finally, divergence becomes so great that different languages come into being, and a language *family* exists where originally there was just one language.

GEOGRAPHICAL LINGUISTICS

Now our topic is geographical linguistics—language in relation to
space. (Diachronic linguistics is Saussure's term for language in
relation to time and it will come in again here.) Saussure says that
the diversity of languages in space is easier to think about than the
diversity of languages in time, but you can be the judge of that for
yourself. He starts his lessons on geographical linguistics by talking
about tendencies: the tendency to think of language as a local cus-
tom, the tendency to assume the superiority of our own language,
the tendency to look for similarities in languages once differences
have been established. He also talks about an impossibility: the
impossibility of ever finding out whether all languages came from
one. There has been too much language change to get an answer to
this question. But this doesn't keep the linguist from comparing languages—those that are very different from each other as well as
those that are similar.

Three things can happen when different languages come together in the same territory:

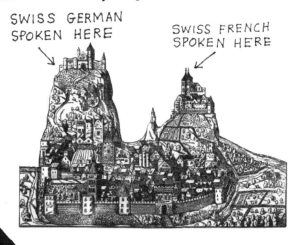

They get mixed together like the ingredients of a cake or a stew. This is what happened to English after the Norman Conquest (1066 and all that). English absorbed elements of the language of the conquering French.

SWISS GERMAN SPOKEN HERE

SWISS FRENCH SPOKEN HERE

They each get used in their own separate piece of the territory, which is the case for French and German in Saussure's bithplace—Switzerland.

EUZKADI ALA IL!!

They co-exist without getting mixed together. In the Basque region of the Pyrenees mountains between France and Spain, French, Spanish and Basque are spoken. At the time of the Roman Empire, languages co-existed this way all around the Mediterranean.

When languages are related, how they differ from each other can be observed and traced back to what unites them. Saussure's big interest here is getting at the cause of the differences. He points out that distance alone does not create differences. Time is the determining factor. If half the speakers of a language were packed off to a new location on the other side of the world, the day they got there they would still be speaking the same way as the people back home. But after decades and centuries the language would have undergone certain changes in the new location AND other changes among the speakers back home. So the unity of related languages is to be found in time alone.

Now what happens in a country where there is just one language and a stable population? To lead into the answer to this question, Saussure reminds us of one of his most basic lessons on linguistics: the sign is changeable. Change in language is inevitable and going on all the time, as we noted in our section above devoted to

 this topic. And this change cannot be uniform over the territory where the language is spoken. How do we know this for a fact? Because there is no record anywhere of any language ever having

changed in exactly the same way everywhere that it is spoken. Here it is visually:

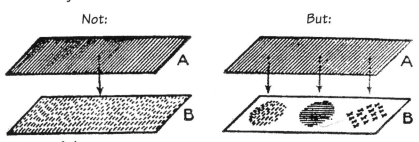

This state of affairs only raises more questions. What is the starting point for the language changes that end up producing different dialects (local speech)? What pattern of changes is involved? To answer these questions, we have to keep two basic facts in mind:

language change takes the form of specific innovations that follow each other one by one AND each of these innovations covers a definite and well marked-out area. If the area happens to be the whole territory where the language is spoken, no dialect differences will be created; if the area covered by the innovation is only part of the territory, dialect differences will begin to emerge.

Now a shift in pronunciation from <u>a</u> to <u>e</u>, for example, can occur on the same territory as a shift in pronunciation from <u>s</u> to <u>z</u>, but in different <u>parts</u> of that territory. There is no way of predicting what direction dialect changes will take when they spread, so if they are all shown together on a map, they make very complicated patterns.

What is the result of this kind of differentiation over time? One language may be spoken throughout a vast area, but as centuries go by and it undergoes local changes everywhere, speakers from the extreme regions will likely not be able to understand each other, whereas speakers in neighboring regions will. Travelling from one region to another, you would notice only limited differences between dialects, but the sum of those differences grows till it finally distinguishes one language from another.

Barking Up the Wrong Syntactic Tree

A dog walked into the Western Union telegraph office, took a blank form and wrote: "woof, woof, woof, woof, woof, woof, woof, woof, woof." The clerk looked over the form and pointed out that there were only nine words, and that for the same price the dog could send an extra "woof." The dog frowned and replied, "that would make no sense at all."

Saussure broke with nineteenth century historical linguistics. He also breaks with the approach to dialect studies as they had been done up to his time. He rejects the idea of dialect areas as perfectly defined and sitting neatly side by side, as they were usually shown on linguistic maps:

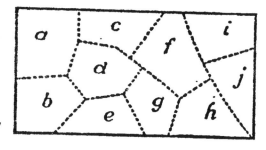

The natural development of dialects does not give these types of results, Saussure says. In fact, he scraps the idea of natural dialects altogether and prefers to say only that there are natural dialect features. There are as many dialects as there are speech communities. (If you remember Professor Henry Higgins in *My Fair Lady* claiming that he could tell where people lived to within a few streets by how they speak, you've got the idea Saussure is trying to get across here.)

What to substitute then for that artificially tidy dialect map? Saussure says there are two choices. A dialect could be defined by one of its features and the map could show the spread of this feature. But this is not a great idea, since the map will wind up showing a boundary of an isolated feature instead of any dialect as it is actually spoken. A better prospect is defining a dialect by the sum of its features and choosing a community of speakers. Now when we choose a second point for a second community of speakers what happens? Instead of the tidy single lines separating them, a number of lines separate them—one for each distinguishing feature of their dialects. We wind up with a map which looks like this:

Now if you think this does not look much like a map, remember the subject is dialect geography and that for now only two speech communities are shown on the map. When other communities are added to make a more complete map, they will be separated from each other by boundaries that look something like this:

A completely complete dialect map would have many such zones marked on it. Not surprisingly, Saussure calls the boundaries defining dialects <u>INNOVATING WAVES</u>, because of their shape, and because they mark the points where innovations occur in the form of the language underlying different dialects. Notice that the waves can almost coincide or overlap. (You can see this clearly on the map where only A and B are shown.) Saussure says that a dialect is defined by a sufficient accumulation of such overlaps.

... how are languages defined?

If this is the method for defining dialects, how are languages defined? Saussure admits that it is hard to say exactly what separates a dialect from a language. Sometimes a dialect takes on the status of a language because a body of literature is written in it. This is what happened for Portuguese and Dutch. A more important factor is understanding: If people do not understand each other's speech, it is agreed that they speak different languages. (If they do understand each other and there are only a few differences in their speech, they speak related dialects.) But languages are like dialects in that innovating waves define them, it's just that the waves show up over a much larger territory for languages than for dialects. And tidy dividing lines between languages are obscured by areas of transition, just as they are for dialects.

BUT! When intermediate dialects disappear, groups of dialects that make up a language do NOT continue merging into each other. Instead, they collide. This happened for Germanic and Slavic languages and many others. What is today the national standard for literary French used to be only the local language of the Ile de France (a former province of north central France, including Paris and the surrounding region). It now extends to all of Frances borders, including the one with Italy, where it comes up against standard Italian, itself originally a dialect spoken only in the region of Tuscany.

How do linguistic waves spread? (Important question for Saussure.) Wouldn't you know it? After giving us ying/yang style oppositions all the way through the <u>CGL</u> (language/speech, signifier/signified, etc.)  Saussure comes up with two opposing forces to answer our latest question. He calls them <u>INTER-COURSE</u> and <u>PROVINCIALISM</u>, but that may not do much for you, so let's call them <u>INTERACTION</u> and <u>INERTIA</u>. Inertia keeps us in our beds, in our houses, in our towns. It also keeps us speaking the way we have always spoken. If nobody ever moved from place to place, the result of inertia, according to Saussure, would be an infinite number of peculiarities in speech. But interaction keeps this from happening. It spreads language and gives it unity.

This unity through interaction comes about in two ways. Saussure's explanation for this, as usual, puts the emphasis on forces that balance each other: there is a negative force that wipes out innovation and keeps dialects from splintering; there is a positive force that promotes unity when an innovation is accepted and spreads. (We are not going to get into a full-scale review of all of Saussure's ideas here, but this one is linked to the lessons on the LINGUISTIC SIGN: because it is arbitrary, it cannot be changed by design; because it is arbitrary, it does change by chance. There is a connection between what Saussure is saying about the double effect of ARBITRARINESS and what he is saying about the double effect of INTERACTION on the unity of language.)

It's because of the spread of a new feature of language permitted by both the ARBITRARINESS of the sign and the INTERACTION principle that Saussure talks about <u>INNOVATING WAVES</u>. The line that describes the boundary of a geographical fact about a dialect is like the leading edge of a wave. (We are not going to get into a full-scale review of all of Saussure's ideas here—honest!—but you might want to check out the fact that he used the idea of a wave in his section on synchronic linguistics. Waves are like the coming together of thought and sound in the LINGUISTIC SIGN.) The waves of language change start at a single point in one dialect and spread out gradually. How these waves spread is different from how the change got started in the first place. At the single point that is its source, the change is taking shape in time alone, but once it starts to spread, time and space both come into play.

It's easy to tell the forces of INTERACTION and INERTIA apart when dealing with a single geographical point such as one village. Any fact about the speech of the village depends on one or the other. Once the linguist looks at a larger territory, where two or more dialects are spoken, it is impossible to say which force is responsible for which feature. Inertia keeps the speakers of this territory from imitating the speech of another territory, but interaction within the territory is also at work and keeps it unified. The interesting little twist that Saussure gives at the end of this lesson is the observation that linguistic change can be studied without taking INERTIA into account. INTERIA is the negative dimension of INTERACTION; it's the INTERACTION within a region of speech communities.

Saussure liked the wave theory of language origins and language groupings, because it helped to correct some mistakes that linguists before him had made in their speculation about language origins and language groupings. The wave theory also helps to understand the causes of language differentiation and the conditions that determine which languages are related. He had more to say about this and about another subject he called RETROSPECTIVE LINGUISTICS, but this is definitely not FOR BEGINNERS!

The Linguistic Graveyard
Latin is a language,
Dead as dead can be,
First it killed the Romans,
Now it's killing me.

This was a popular jingle in the days (not so long ago) when schools still taught Latin. Yes, Latin is dead, except in the Vatican, where resident scholars still coin new words to add to the language, if the Pope's latest encyclical so requires. Over the ages Latin has been joined in the linguistic graveyard by many others. Here is the story of Akkadian, an extinct language of Iraq.

Akkadian belonged to the vast family of languages spoken in the Near East, including Arabic, Hebrew, and Aramaic, a family known as Semitic, because the speakers of these languages were descended from Noah's son Shem (or Sem). Akkadian was a ruling language in Iraq and Syria in the second millennium B.C.E. Clay tablets inscribed with Akkadian cuneiform script (*cuneiform* comes from the Latin word *cuneus*, meaning "wedge-shaped") preserved some of the world's most ancient literature, including the Epic of Gilgamesh (a tale of a semi-divine hero and his quest for the secret of eternal life) and myths of the Creation and the Flood with close counterparts in Hebrew Biblical texts.

When Aramaic and Greek replaced Akkadian, it fell into disuse and may have been forgotten forever, if inscriptions in its exotic, spiky script on clay tablets had not been discovered by travelling adventurers in the 17th century. It was only then that scholars took up the daunting challenge of deciphering this ancient language. The texts of those tablets that survived two thousand years — literature,

chronicles, business records, school exercises, and even recipes — have given us a rich record of Akkadian culture.

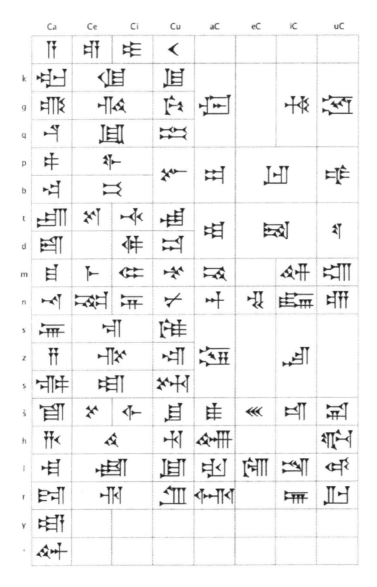

	Ca	Ce	Ci	Cu	aC	eC	iC	uC
	𒀹	𒀸	𒀾	𒀼				
k	𒅗	𒆠	𒆤					
g	𒂵	𒄀	𒄉	𒄘			𒅅	𒊼
q	𒋡	𒆥	𒆕					
p	𒉺	𒉿		𒁍	𒀊	𒅁	𒅁	𒌒
b	𒁀	𒁁						
t	𒋫	𒋼	𒋾	𒌇	𒀜	𒀉		𒌆
d	𒁕		𒁲	𒁺				
m	𒈠	𒈨	𒈪	𒈬	�am		𒅎	𒌝
n	𒈾	𒉈	𒉌	𒉡	𒀭	𒂗	𒅔	𒌦
s	𒊓	�006	𒋛					
z	𒍝	𒍣	𒍢	𒍪		𒄑		
ṣ	𒍍	𒍤	𒍥					
š	𒊭	𒊺	𒅆	𒋗	𒀸	𒌍	𒅖	𒍑
h	𒄩	𒃶	𒄭	𒄷			𒄴	
l	𒆷	𒇷	𒇷	𒇻	𒀠	𒂖	𒅋	𒌌
r	𒊏	𒊑	�878	𒊒			𒅕	𒌨
y	𒅀							
ʾ	𒄴							

We know too that Akkadian achieved the status of one of the first international languages in the domains of both commerce and diplomacy in the Middle East, because Akkadian texts from as early as the second millennium B.C.E. have been found in Egypt, for example, well away from the areas where the language was in everyday use.

Pity the brave linguists who set about cracking the code of the Akkadian writing system, containing over a thousand symbols. Some of these stood for syllabes (groups of sounds), some for a whole word or for a concept. Many of the symbols developed from others used in the writing systems of unrelated languages.

LINGUISTICS AND PHILOSOPHY

Another Kind of **Semantics**

Semantics, as we have seen, is the branch of linguistics that analyzes meaning, but *general* **semantics** is not part of linguistics in the conventional sense of analysis of language. Or at least it is not

COUNT KORZYBSKI

limited to that. *General* **semantics** was the invention of a Polish-born nobleman, Count Alfred Korzybski (1879-1950), who emigrated to the United States. While Korzybski was interested in language and problems of communication, he developed *general* **semantics** in the 1930s as an applied form of philosophy, intended to explain the workings of the nervous system and to train people in the more efficient use of it. In 1943, Korzybski founded the Institute of General **Semantics** and the International Society for General

Semantics. The Society's journal, *Et cetera*, reflects little of Korzybski's work today, but it is a lively publication and retains a focus on communication and education.

Bedevilled by a Beetle

Like many other subjects that eventually spun off on their own, linguistics had its first home in the traditions of investigation and debate that are the domain of philosophers, and we mentioned Aristotle in "Linguistics Then and Now" above. Let's fast forward to a key figure in the evolution of the twentieth century philosophical movement called *philosophy of mind*, the intellectual giant whose work is credited with bringing to philosophy a new direction called *the linguistic turn*. This was Ludwig Wittgenstein (1889-1951).

ARISTOTLE

WITTGENSTEIN

His argument against dualism (the philosophical position that accepts a basic division of the universe into mind and matter) involved a colorful analogy with an imaginary *beetle box*. Here is what Witters (Wittgenstein's nickname among the really savvy) asked his readers to imagine: everybody has a box containing something called a "beetle." (It turns out later that the key word here is not "beetle" but "something.") Nobody is allowed to look inside anyone else's box, but everyone claims to know what a beetle is just from what is in their own box. (It turns out later that the key word here is not "beetle" but "what.") Now if the word "beetle" is used among beetle box owners, it cannot be for the purpose of naming a thing, because nobody knows what is in anyone else's box. (The "something" in the box may even be nothing.)

Use of a word and naming of a thing have to be separate, and that's the catch for dualists, if they concede that words such as "pain," for example, have a use. The term is shared by language users, but direct knowledge of it is not. It's as inaccessible as all those beetles nobody is allowed to peek at. In use, "beetle" is not (the name of) something, but it is not nothing either (even if there is nothing in the box). Using the word makes it something but does not make it the name of something. The story goes that beetle boxes began springing up on people's mantels in Cambridge and Oxford to indicate that they knew about Wittgenstein's posthumously published *Philosophical Investigations*.

A Linguistic Bestiary

(1) Witter's Lion

Among the well-known quotations from Wittgenstein's writings is the passage that says: "If a lion could talk, we could not understand him." Perhaps our philosopher was thinking about the fact that biological differences exist between the perceptual mechanisms of humans and animals. This *is* a fact and needs to be taken account of in describing the dif-

ferences between human ways of communicating and the exchanges that take place among birds, bees, and beasts. Perhaps he had something more subtle in mind.

A lot of ink has flowed in the discussion over Wittgenstein's observation, and a lot of complex issues are involved, but there are some valuable lessons even for beginners in thinking about what the old boy meant, and especially in examining both his suppositions and the lesson he may have intended to illustrate with his memorable example. Let's put it in the form of questions that connect with basics in linguistics. And remember that here the questions are more important than the answers:

i) If a lion could talk, why could we not record what he says, just as linguists do in their field work with unknown languages, and work out the analysis of lion language bit by bit, **phoneme** by **phoneme**, *morpheme* by morpheme, structure by structure?

ii) Did Wittgenstein believe that the interplay of speech (what is said) and language (what can be said), a characteristic of all natural human languages, and deeply ingrained in our predispositon to social meaning-making might not exist for that chatty lion?

iii) All the languages in the world of humans are translatable, even if only roughly in some cases, into all other languages, so would it be impossible to translate lionese into human language?

Wittgenstein began with an *if*, and we have to add another one here: if the answer to our last two questions is *yes*, then our philosopher may have intended to offer a lesson about a universal feature of human language that distinguishes it from other possible forms of language. Philosopher Steven Burns puts it in these terms: if we go back to the context where Wittgenstein made his observation, we see that it requires an account of perception (in particular, of objectivity and subjectivity in the case of *seeing-as*) and of meaning in relation to perception.

And this brings us back to the phenomenon of social meaning-making, precisely what could keep us from understanding the lion. If he is not a social animal like ourselves, he may not even be speaking, even if he could trick us into supposing that he is speaking to us (here we are back to Wittgenstein's *if*).

(2) Parrots Are No Good with Paraphrases or Paradigms

A linguistic lesson beyond Wittgenstein's is brought home when we look closely at the not-so-amazing ability of parrots to say just about anything that their humans will teach them to say. Parrots are mimics, but they have no linguistic skills other than being able to repeat fragments of language with fine accuracy. Once your parrot learns "Polly wants a cracker," that phrase will always come out in the same form. Saying "I would sure like to have a soda biscuit" is not an option for the parrot.

The ability of humans to master a language involves paraphrase skills (re-expressing a message in other terms), and this, in turn, involves acquiring the ability to select among items in a language system that are related in form and meaning (*paradigms*) and then to combine them properly (look back at the sections on *morphology* and **syntax**) to make sentences that make sense. Our parrot, of course, does not know his **syntax** from his **semantics**.

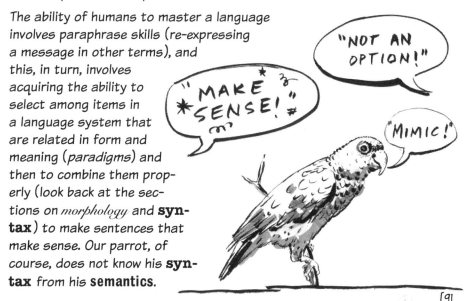

The parrot's phrase, paraphrase, and a pared down phrase

A missionary visiting a tribal community gives a very long sermon. One of his anecdotes goes on for nearly half an hour. Then the interpreter stands up, says four words, and all the listeners roar with laughter. The missionary is baffled. How is it possible that his complicated story can be translated into four words? What kind of amazing language do these people speak? He asks the interpreter how he managed to pack the whole story into four words. The interpreter replies, "Story too long. I say. 'He tell joke-laugh!'"

ANTHROPOLOGICAL LINGUISTICS...

...focuses on the link between language and culture. Cultural anthropologists (as opposed to physical anthropologists, who confine
themselves to looking at stones and bones) learn the languages of
the people they study for the practical purpose of communicating
with them, but they also examine the language for clues to the culture expressed through it. In the USA, it was Franz Boas (go back
and have a look at "A Flurry of Words for Snow") who pioneered and
emphasized the study of native American cultures.

His student Edward Sapir entrenched this approach and set the direction that American linguistics would take for decades before Noam Chomsky came along to upset the anthropological applecart.

In Britain, it was the Polish-born anthropologist Bronislaw Malinowski who gave the study of language its anthropological thrust in the early twentieth century. Nearly eighty years after its first publication, his essay on meaning in relation to culture continues to be reprinted as a supplement to Ogden's & Richards's *The Meaning of Meaning.* Malinowski ended his career in America, but his ideas exerted a big influence on John Rupert Firth (1890-1960), acknowledged as the father of linguistics in Britain. New areas of linguistics have opened up on its borderlands with sociology, psychology, and other disciplines, but anthropological linguistics remains an active field of research. The cultural anthropologists who work in linguistics were by no means left in the dust by the stampede to theoretical linguistics. Lively publications continue to appear, for example, on the ever-popular topics of kinship terms and color names.

Kinship Terms

Studying the expression of terms for *mother, father, brother, sister,* (etc.) in your language of choice has at least one big advantage over other areas of the vocabulary. Even if a culture has a very complex system of names for cousins, let us say (separate words for father's brother's son, father's sister's son, mother's sister's daughter, etc.), there are clearly defined limits on which words need to go into the linguist's analysis to give a complete picture. Starting with domains like kinship makes it easier for the linguist to get a handle on a language and its culture. Here is an example of kin terms from Swedish:

FARMOR

FARFAR

MORFAR

MORMOR

farfar - grandfather (=father's father)
farmor - grandfather (=mother's father)
mormor - grandmother (=mother's mother)
morfar - grandmother (=father's mother)

These words also give us an example of what linguists call *morphological* motivation (look back to our section on *morphology*). This means that the parts of the word "add up" to the meaning of the whole (it is a fact and clear to the speakers of Swedish that *farfar* means the *far* of your *far*; compare English, where *grandfather* is not necessarily a father who is grand).

Kinship terms vary greatly from one language to another. Comparisons with English show both simpler and more complex organization. Parallel to the example of the Swedish grandparents above, we discover that many languages distinguish between 'father's brother' and 'mother's brother,' whereas English has only *uncle*. But whereas English makes a distinction between *niece* and *nephew*, some languages make do with a single word for both, leaving the masculine/feminine contrast unexpressed. In some cases, one word covers not only *niece* and *nephew* but also *grandson* and *granddaughter*. And whereas both men and women have *sisters* in English, in Basque a man has an *arreba*, while a woman has an *ahizpa*. In Seneca, an age distinction is made explicit in the kin terms, giving different words for *older sister* and *younger sister*.

Recent publications relate kinship terminology to other social phenomena, as well as touching on the role of language in cognitive development, dialectology, loanwords, language change, universal features. These are rich additions to the accurate interpretation of culture, which was, and remains, one of the primary purposes of studying kin terms.

What is the chief interest of kinship for linguistics? If, as is often said, every linguist is at heart a collector, nowhere do the butterflies of language showcase in a more spectacular way than in kin terms. Except, perhaps, for...

Color Names

Like words for kin, those for color appeal to linguists as an area of study because it appears inherently tidy. After decades of study, things look a little more complicated here than they did at first, but color is still a lot less fuzzy a domain than, say, the expression of beauty, art, democracy, fashion, etc., though brave linguists have tackled these subjects too.

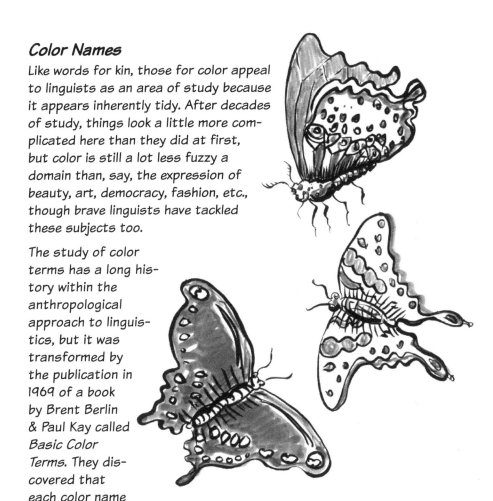

The study of color terms has a long history within the anthropological approach to linguistics, but it was transformed by the publication in 1969 of a book by Brent Berlin & Paul Kay called *Basic Color Terms*. They discovered that each color name has a consistent focus and thus removed variable category boundaries for color names among languages as an obstacle to a theory of semantic universals in this domain. Berlin & Kay claimed these universals take the form of a set of sequentially applicable rules:

Rule 1: All languages have terms for black and white.

Rule 2: If a language has only three names for colors, the third will be a term for the color red.

yellow

green

Rule 3: If the language has only four names for colors, the fourth will be a term for green or yellow.

In other words, only in the case of a language more complex than one described by rule 3 will the distinction appear among red, orange, yellow, or among green, blue, and violet.

Berlin & Kay found both supporters and detractors. Both camps offer irrefutable empirical evidence for *and* against the Berlin & Kay thesis. Some researchers have designed experiments to compensate for what they see as deficiencies of method in Berlin & Kay. Some offer improved procedures for investigating color terms, in this case providing support for Berlin & Kay. Ten years after the publication of his original study with Berlin, Kay, working with another partner, concluded that the structure of the color lexicon is a physiologically determined phenomenon, thereby strengthening the claim for semantic universals in this domain. Debate over the Berlin & Kay thesis continues into its fourth decade.

With the suggestion that universals of perception exist in spite of differences among languages, the Berlin and Kay rules for color terms challenge the so-called Sapir-Whorf hypothesis of linguistic relativity. American linguist Edward Sapir (1884-1939) spoke of the "thought-grooves" that he viewed as inseparable from the language of the thinker, and his student Benjamin Lee Whorf (1897-1941) pursued this view.

EDWARD SAPIR

He sharpened his teacher's metaphor (if we may be permitted to mix our own) to the point that encouraged a somewhat overstated in-a-nutshell version of Sapir-Whorf: the structure of our language determines the way we perceive the world. Notice carefully how this statement differs from Wittgenstein's observation on the connection between language and world view in *A Final Word* below.

The linguistic relativity hypothesis did not begin with Sapir-Whorf. Centuries earlier, scholars began speculating on the connections among language, mind, perception, and culture. A notable example was the eighteenth century German who held down at least three jobs as statesman, philosopher, and linguist (linguists, we noted earlier, were called *philologists* in those days), Wilhelm von Humboldt (1767-1835).

Benjamin Lee Whorf

The structure of our language determines the way we perceive the world

LINGUISTICS AND BEYOND

From Structuralism to Poststructuralism

The approach to linguistics which views language as a structured system is called *structuralism*. Up until the twentieth century, linguists dealt with language as a collection of individual elements: speech sounds, words, grammatical word-endings, etc. Just as the twentieth century dawned, the Swiss genius Ferdinand de Saussure, whose work we have already mentioned a few times above, started linguistics on the road to a whole new outlook and methods. His *Course in General Linguistics (CGL)* made the case that the best way to view language is as a structured system.

SWISS GENIUS SAUSSURE

He put the emphasis on how each element of language is related to other elements, because he saw this as a way to correct a lot of errors that had been made by earlier linguists who never looked at the big picture. Saussure's approach came to be known as *structuralism*, though he did not use the term himself, nor is the term *structure* very prominent in the *CGL*.

JACQUES DERRIDA

From Saussure's teachings, structuralism eventually emerged as the dominant approach to linguistics among European scholars. A structuralist orientation to linguistics also developed in the USA under Edward Sapir and Leonard Bloomfield, but are recognizably distinct from Saussure's original teachings.

The legendary U.S. philosopher, mathematician, and inventor of the geodesic dome, Buckminster Fuller, once said that the disciples of Christ took his powerful teachings and turned them into the language of Humpty-Dumpty. Many believe that much the same thing happened when the principles set out by the granddaddy of linguistics, Ferdinand de Saussure, were used and interpreted by Jacques Derrida, who is generally acknowledged as being the founder of post-structuralism (also called deconstruction)—an attempt to correct the perceived shortcomings of structuralism.

Derrida argues that there are three weak points in Saussure's teachings: his idealism, his emphasis on spoken language, and his use of paired opposites to describe features of language.
By idealism Derrida means the view that language does not create meanings but expresses pre-existing ones. Derrida disregards Sausurre's key point that the language-system mediates between thought and sound. Both thought and sound are formless, Saussure said, until they are linked and acquire form through the creation of those links—called signs. There are no pre-existing meanings in this view, as Derrida believes.

Derrida makes the concept of *difference* all important, as it is for Saussure, except that he does not keep the complementary term *opposition*. But he does follow Saussure in making *system* a key idea. On the basis of *system* and *difference*, Derrida develops the concept of *archi-writing*. This is supposed to be a system consisting of pure differences that underlies speaking AND writing. Saussure did not recognize such a system, according to Derrida, because he held a prejudiced view of writing as nothing more than a way of representing speech. To call Saussure's view of writing a prejudice is to disregard his purpose in developing a new approach to linguistics, namely avoiding the confusion and errors that marked the work of earlier linguists, who had always limited themselves to written texts.

Derrida rejects Saussure's use of complementary pairs of terms such as *associative relations* and *syntagmatic relations*. This pair, in particular, is related to the even more fundamental one of *absence/presence*, which Derrida refuses.

The whole project of eliminating such pairs is unnecessary when we recall that Saussure ended his lesson on syntagmatic relations and associative relations by showing how they interact. They are defined independently but they function interdependently. Since definitions are particularly subject to the endless play of signifiers (a normal state of affairs, according to the post-structuralist view), there is no point in objecting to their provisionally independent status in Saussurian linguistics. Saussure moved beyond all his dualities himself. In this sense, he deconstructed structuralism more than half a century before Derrida.

A FINAL WORD

Wittgenstein said that the limits of our language are the limits of our world. The great Canadian literary critic Northrop Frye was talking about the same thing when he said that the best reason to study a language other than the one you have spoken from birth is to disengage your thought processes from what he called "the swaddling clothes of their native **syntax**." If we can get over that "ever eerier feeling" that Ogden Nash speaks of in the quotation we used at the start of this book, we can use linguistics to stretch our understanding of the world too.

****

APPENDIX #1 Up for the Count

Let's have a look at a common initiation ritual for beginners in linguistics: learning the numbers from one to ten in different languages. This little exercise does not show anything linguistically, but for many teachers of linguistics, it is a favorite way to introduce their students to the diversity of the world's languages and to give practice in hearing, pronouncing, and transcribing unfamiliar data.

It's a bit too early for you to have mastered *phonetic* transcription, so the examples below are given in conventional English spelling, even though this makes for a certain loss of accuracy in indicating their pronunciation.

Bai (China)
yi, go, sa, shi, ngur, fer, chi, bia, jiu, dser

Balinese (Indonesia)
sa, dua (or kalih), talu (or tiga), pat, lima, nam, pitu, kutus (or ulu), sia, dasa

Ukrainian (Ukraine)
odin, dva, tri, chotiri, pyat', shests', syem, vosyem, devyats', desyats'

Bikol (Philippines)
saro', duwa, tulo, apat, lima, anom, pito, walo, siyam, sampulo'

Bislama (Vanuata, formerly the New Hebrides)
wan, tu, tri, fo, faev, sikis, seven, et, naen, ten

Welsh (Wales)
un, dau/dwy, tri/tair, pedwar/pedair, pump, chwech, saith, wyth, naw, deg

Manchu (northeastern China, fewer than 1,000 surviving speakers)
emu, juwe, ilan, duin, sunja, niggun, nadan, jakon, uyun, juwan

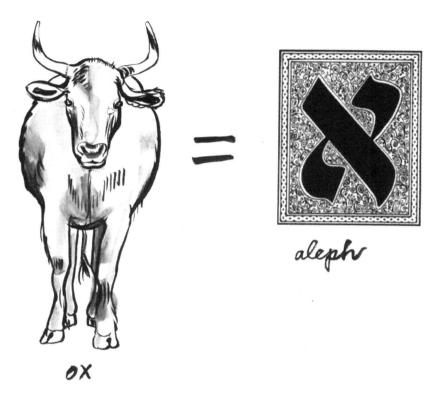

OX

aleph

Historically, A/a is not for *apple* but for *ox*. How can this be? Our alphabet, the Latin alphabet, derives from the Greek alphabet, but its hoariest ancestor is ancient Proto-Sinaitic, where A/a began life as a stylized drawing of an ox. In between came Phoenician and Hebrew, and in all cases, the alphabets of these languages begin with the ox (called *aleph* in Phoenician and *aleph* or *aluph* in Hebrew). The animal's privileged position reflects its central importance in an agricultural society and as a symbol of strength. The upright horns on the ox's head turned east by the time the *aleph* passed into Greek as *alpha* (?) and then headed (pun intended) due south in the transformation into Latin A.

The story of B begins with Proto-Sinaitic *bayit* (house) and moves to *beth* (house) in Phoenician and Hebrew before becoming Greek *beta* (?). The straight lines of the original floor plan of the house gave way to loops and curved lines, and, like *alpha*, *beta* changed direction.

But the much bigger change that came along the way from Hebrew to Greek was in the loss of meanings. Beginning with Greek, the names of the letters of the alphabet refer only to themselves. No more ox, house, camel, door, or any of the other familiar things from everyday life that lent their shapes and names to make up the bits and pieces of the older alphabets.

> The pun on *alphabet* invented by that great linguist James Joyce in *Finnegans Wake* is *allforabit.*

This was a huge change that gave the new alphabet (? + ?) tremendous power. All the visual reminders of oxen, houses, etc., disappeared and the whole focus of the alphabet shifted to language itself. On the one hand, all the associations of meaning for the objects originally linked to letter names were eliminated—traded in, as it were, for nothing more than the sound at the beginning of the names of those objects (all for a bit). On the other hand, that left the new sound-letters free to combine with each other in any number of ways to create new meaning (all for a bit).

APPENDIX #3 Women's Script

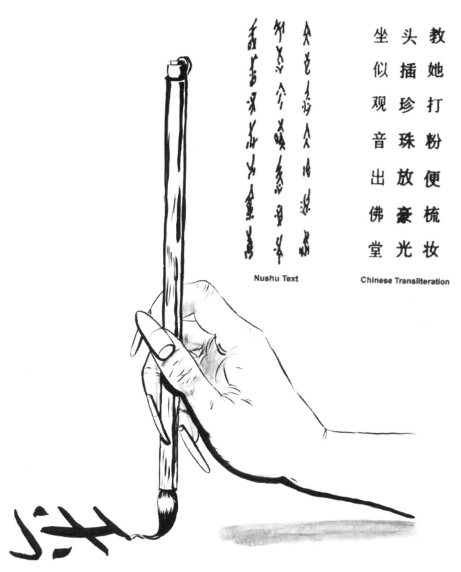

Nushu Text

Chinese Transliteration

坐	头	教
似	插	她
观	珍	打
音	珠	粉
出	放	便
佛	豪	梳
堂	光	妆

The women of Jiangyong in southern China have kept an extraordinary secret since the days of the ancient Song Dynasty. According to legend, it was an emperor's concubine who invented *nushu* (women's script), allowing her to pour out the forbidden expression of her loneliness in letters to her sisters without revealing it to male eyes. Nushu is related to ancient Chinese script, predating the time of Qin Shihuang, who was responsible for the unification of China and became the first Chinese emperor in 221 B.C. Qin's drive for unification eliminated all local written languages, and the penalty for creating new ones was death for the innovator, her family, and nine related families. But nushu escaped the attention of authorities, because women and women's activities had no official status, and the secret script survived. Ironically, access to education and increased freedom to work and travel for women in modern China have all but ensured the extinction of the script that gave them a powerful bond for centuries. (A traditional proverb in nushu says "Beside a well one does not thirst; beside sisters one does not despair.") The only three remaining women of Jiangyong who know the script have taught it to no one, because no one wishes to learn it. Even though some dedicated scholar may rise to the challenge of preserving its texts, nushu will become a linguistic fossil.

APPENDIX #4 Historical Linguistics

Historical linguistics studies changes in language. It is usually said to have begun in the late eighteenth century, when Sir William Jones (1746-94), formerly tutor to an ancestor of the late Princess Diana of Wales, began to document the previously unnoticed resemblance between Latin and Greek and the ancient Sanskrit language. This was the first step in defining and describing the vast family of languages known as Indo-European, stretching across the two continents identified in its name, a group in which all members are the offspring of a linguistic Adam. Historical linguistics, with its emphasis on groupings and affinities, classification and comparison, dominated linguistics until Ferdinand de Saussure came along and proposed that the historical approach (he called it *diachronic*) be balanced by the study of language as a system (he called this the *synchronic* approach). Instead of achieving the balance Saussure was looking for, twentieth century linguists went overboard on synchronic studies. But today the search for principles underlying linguistic change is being revitalized, and linguists are looking in particular at the link between that change and linguistic variation (see our section on *geographical linguistics*).

Appendix #5 More About Phonetics
SOME SOUNDS OF ENGLISH
(sʌm sowndz ʌv ɛŋglɪʃ)

You see in brackets above which of the letters in standard spelling carry over from our heading "ome Sounds of English" to its phonetic transcription.

What's missing?

1) all the vowels, because standard spelling does not consistently show how to pronounce the twenty of more vowels that occur in most variants of English;

2) some consonants, because the *n* in *English* is not the *n* of *ran* but of *rang* and the *sh* in *English* is not two sounds but one.

What's different?

1) the final *-s* of *sounds* is transcribed *z*, because it is pronounced as *z*;

2) *v* and not *f* in the transcription of *of*, because it is pronounced as *v*.

Now if we fill in, using the International Phonetic Alphabet (remember that the principle of this alphabet is one symbol for one sound and a different symbol for every sound), we get the full transcription as above.

THE REST OF THE SOUNDS OF ENGLISH

And for those of you who can't get enough phonetics, here is the complete table of the basic symbols for consonants and vowels in the International Phonetics Alphabet. Our examples have been limited to English, but remember that this alphabet was designed so that linguists could accurately transcribe the spoken version of any language in the world. To do this, in some cases, you need some additional symbols not shown in this table.

THE INTERNATIONAL PHONETIC ALPHABET (revised to 2005)

CONSONANTS (PULMONIC)

	Bilabial	Labiodental	Dental	Alveolar	Postalveolar	Retroflex	Palatal	Velar	Uvular	Pharyngeal	Glottal
Plosive	p b			t d		ʈ ɖ	c ɟ	k g	q ɢ		ʔ
Nasal	m	ɱ		n		ɳ	ɲ	ŋ	N		
Trill	B			r					R		
Tap or Flap		ⱱ		ɾ		ɽ					
Fricative	ɸ β	f v	θ ð	s z	ʃ ʒ	ʂ ʐ	ç ʝ	x ɣ	χ ʁ	ħ ʕ	h ɦ
Lateral fricative				ɬ ɮ							
Approximant		ʋ		ɹ		ɻ	j	ɰ			
Lateral approximant				l		ɭ	ʎ	L			

Where symbols appear in pairs, the one to the right represents a voiced consonant. Shaded areas denote articulations judged impossible.

CONSONANTS (NON-PULMONIC)

Clicks		Voiced implosives		Ejectives	
ʘ	Bilabial	ɓ	Bilabial	ʼ	Examples:
ǀ	Dental	ɗ	Dental/alveolar	pʼ	Bilabial
ǃ	(Post)alveolar	ʄ	Palatal	tʼ	Dental/alveolar
ǂ	Palatoalveolar	ɠ	Velar	kʼ	Velar
ǁ	Alveolar lateral	ʛ	Uvular	sʼ	Alveolar fricative

OTHER SYMBOLS

ʍ Voiceless labial-velar fricative
w Voiced labial-velar approximant
ɥ Voiced labial-palatal approximant
H Voiceless epiglottal fricative
ʕ Voiced epiglottal fricative
ʡ Epiglottal plosive

ɕ ʑ Alveolo-palatal fricatives
ɺ Voiced alveolar lateral flap
ɧ Simultaneous ʃ and x

Affricates and double articulations can be represented by two symbols joined by a tie bar if necessary.

k͡p t͡s

DIACRITICS Diacritics may be placed above a symbol with a descender, e.g. ŋ̊

̥	Voiceless	n̥ d̥	̤	Breathy voiced	b̤ a̤	̪	Dental	t̪ d̪
̬	Voiced	s̬ t̬	̰	Creaky voiced	b̰ a̰	̺	Apical	t̺ d̺
ʰ	Aspirated	tʰ dʰ	̼	Linguolabial	t̼ d̼	̻	Laminal	t̻ d̻
̹	More rounded	ɔ̹	ʷ	Labialized	tʷ dʷ	̃	Nasalized	ẽ
̜	Less rounded	ɔ̜	ʲ	Palatalized	tʲ dʲ	ⁿ	Nasal release	dⁿ
̟	Advanced	u̟	ˠ	Velarized	tˠ dˠ	ˡ	Lateral release	dˡ
̠	Retracted	e̠	ˤ	Pharyngealized	tˤ dˤ	̚	No audible release	d̚
̈	Centralized	ë	̴	Velarized or pharyngealized	ɫ			
̽	Mid-centralized	̽e̽	̝	Raised	e̝	(ɹ̝ = voiced alveolar fricative)		
̩	Syllabic	n̩	̞	Lowered	e̞	(β̞ = voiced bilabial approximant)		
̯	Non-syllabic	e̯	̘	Advanced Tongue Root	e̘			
˞	Rhoticity	ɚ a˞	̙	Retracted Tongue Root	e̙			

VOWELS

	Front	Central	Back
Close	i • y	ɨ • ʉ	ɯ • u
		ɪ ʏ ʊ	
Close-mid	e • ø	ɘ • ɵ	ɤ • o
		ə	
Open-mid	ɛ • œ	ɜ • ɞ	ʌ • ɔ
	æ	ɐ	
Open	a • ɶ		ɑ • ɒ

Where symbols appear in pairs, the one to the right represents a rounded vowel.

SUPRASEGMENTALS

ˈ Primary stress
ˌ Secondary stress ˌfoʊnəˈtɪʃən
ː Long eː
ˑ Half-long eˑ
̆ Extra-short ĕ
| Minor (foot) group
‖ Major (intonation) group
. Syllable break ɹi.ækt
‿ Linking (absence of a break)

TONES AND WORD ACCENTS

LEVEL			CONTOUR		
e̋ or	˥	Extra high	ě or	˩˥	Rising
é	˦	High	ê	˥˩	Falling
ē	˧	Mid	e᷄	˦˥	High rising
è	˨	Low	e᷅	˩˨	Low rising
ȅ	˩	Extra low	e᷈	˧˦˧	Rising falling
↓	Downstep		↗	Global rise	
↑	Upstep		↘	Global fall	

Courtesy of the International Phonetic Association (Department of Theoretical and Applied Linguistics, School of English, Aristotle University of Thessaloniki, Thessaloniki 54124, GREECE)

Explanation of terms used:

The line across the top of the table refers to the organs involved in the production of speech. Reading from left to right, we see **where** sounds are produced, moving from front to back in terms of anatomical parts.

The lefthand column describes **how** sounds are produced in the case of the consonants and **degree of closure** of the mouth in the case of vowels.

Plosive (think of *explosive*) refers to any consonant produced by temporary blockage of air coming from the lungs followed by a release.

TO LEARN MORE, PICK UP THESE OTHER FOR BEGINNERS® BOOKS

CHOMSKY
FOR BEGINNERS®

Written by David Cogswell • Illustrated by Paul Gordon
ISBN 978-1-934389-17-1 (1-934389-17-X) • 160 PAGES
$14.95 (CANADIAN $16.95)

DECONSTRUCTION
FOR BEGINNERS®

Written by Jim Powell • Illustrated by Joe Lee
ISBN 978-1-934389-26-3 (1-934389-26-9) • 168 PAGES
$14.95 (CANADIAN $16.95)

DERRIDA
FOR BEGINNERS®

Written by Jim Powell • Illustrated by Joe Lee
ISBN 978-1-934389-26-3 (1-934389-26-9) • 168 PAGES
$14.95 (CANADIAN $16.95)

About the Author

W. Terrence Gordon has published more than twenty books, including *Saussure For Beginners* and *McLuhan For Beginners*. He is currently at work on a book about James Joyce and a biographical fiction about the legendary linguist Charles Kay Ogden. When he is not busy writing or teaching, Gordon photographs the haunting beauty of Nova Scotia, Canada, where he has lived since the 1970s.

About the Illustrator

Susan Willmarth was born in New Mexico and moved in the early '70's to New York City. Since graduating from Parsons School of Design, she has worked as a free-lance editorial illustrator for Push Pin Press Books, Edward Booth-Clibborn editions, *New York Magazine*, The Open Society, Writers and Readers Publishing, and now For Beginners LLC. Past work includes *Black History For Beginners* and *McLuhan For Beginners*. She lives in Manhattan with her bicycle.